Growing Up Smart
Nurturing Early Childhood in the Age of AI

Delilah Gonzales, Ed.D and Ingrid Haynes, Ph.D.

"Growing Up Smart: Nurturing Early Childhood in the Age of AI"

www.emerginglearnersliteracyfoundation.org

All rights reserved. No part of this publication may be reproduced, distributed, or transmitted in any form or by any means, including photocopying, recording, or other electronic or mechanical methods, without the prior written permission of the publisher.

First Edition: Emerging Learners Literacy Foundation Publisher

www.emerginglearnersliteracyfoundation.org

Emerging Learners Literacy Foundation

The mission of Emerging Learners Literacy Foundation is to promote the advancement of the early childhood literacy learner, educator, family and community stakeholders through language and literacy development, social and emotional learning, cultural awareness and community networking. We believe in the importance of developing the early childhood literacy learner in a well-rounded wholeness. Our ultimate goal is to effectively produce a successful child, rooted in a successful family, linking a successful home and which builds a successful community.

Acknowledgement

We would like to extend our heartfelt gratitude to all those who have contributed to the completion of this project. We acknowledge the support and assistance provided by numerous individuals and organizations throughout its development.

We appreciate the guidance and insights shared by experts in the fields of early childhood education, linguistics, and artificial intelligence. Their expertise has enriched our understanding and shaped the direction of our work.

We are also thankful for the resources and facilities provided by academic institutions, which have facilitated our research efforts and enabled us to explore complex topics in depth.

Furthermore, we recognize the encouragement and support received from colleagues, friends, and family members. Their unwavering belief in our endeavors has been a constant source of motivation.

Lastly, we express our appreciation to the broader academic community for their ongoing contributions to knowledge and innovation. It is through their collective efforts that progress is made possible in diverse fields of study.

This project stands as a testament to the collaborative spirit and dedication of all those involved, and we are grateful for the opportunity to contribute to the advancement of scholarship in our respective domains.

About the Authors

Dr. Delilah Gonzales is a distinguished researcher and thought leader in the field of early childhood education, with a doctorate in Early Childhood Education from University of Memphis. Dr. Gonzales has dedicated her career to advancing the understanding and responsible deployment of AI technologies in early childhood settings.

As an advocate for interdisciplinary collaboration, Dr. Gonzales has contributed to numerous research projects that bridge the realms of early childhood education, technology, ethics, and policy. Her work has been instrumental in shaping public discourse on the ethical, social, and educational implications of AI adoption in early childhood education.

Dr. Delilah Gonzales is the founder and director of the Emerging Learning Foundation, an organization dedicated to advancing early childhood literacy. The foundation promotes language and literacy development, social-emotional learning, cultural awareness, and community networking for learners, educators, families, and community stakeholders.

Ingrid Haynes, Ph.D. is a dedicated researcher and educator in the field of linguistics, holding a degree from the University of Mississippi. With a passion for language and communication, Ingrid's academic journey has equipped her with a deep understanding of linguistic theory and its practical applications, including its intersection with artificial intelligence (AI).

With a Ph. D in linguistics fromthe University of Mississippi,Dr. Haynes is committed to sharing her knowledge and insights with others. As an educator, she strives to inspire curiosity and critical thinking in teachers administrators, parents and community stakeholders fostering a deeper appreciation for the complexity and diversity of human language and its interaction with AI technologies.

Dr. Haynes serves as the founder and director of the National Literacy Institute, which is dedicated to fostering collaboration among literacy service providers, foundations, businesses, school districts, and other community partners. The institute's purpose is to ensure that children attain proficient reading, writing, and communication skills, essential life skills that empower them to succeed. Through strategic partnerships and initiatives, the National Literacy Institute strives to equip children with the literacy tools necessary to thrive in today's world.

"Growing Up Smart: Nurturing Early Childhood in the Age of AI"

Table of Contents

Chapter 1 11

An Introduction to the World of Artificial Intelligence

Setting the Stage: Early Childhood and the Emergence of AI

The Significance of Early Childhood Development

Chapter 2 16

Understanding AI Basic

What Is AI?

AI's Impact on Society

AI in Education and Child Development

Evolution of AI in Education:

Applications of AI in Education:

Benefits of AI in Education

Conclusion

Chapter 3 26

The Developing Mind: Early Childhood Cognitive Development

Overview of Cognitive Development in Early Childhood

How AI Influences Cognitive Skills

Cognitive Evolution: The AI Influence

Figure 1

AI-Assisted Learning Tools for Cognitive Development

Chapter 4 33

Social and Emotional Development in the Digital Age

Importance of Social and Emotional Skills in Early Childhood

"Growing Up Smart: Nurturing Early Childhood in the Age of AI"

Challenges and Opportunities of AI in Social and Emotional Learning

Balancing Screen Time and Human Interaction

Chapter 5 39

Language Acquisition and AI

Language Development Milestones in Early Childhood

AI's Role in Language Learning

Ethics and Concerns in Language Acquisition with AI

Chapter 6 47

Play, Creativity, and AI

The Vital Role of Play in Early Childhood

AI and Creative Play

Fostering Creativity in a Digital World

Chapter 7 55

Parenting in the AI Era

Parental Guidance in a Digital Age

Strategies for Navigating AI's Influence on Parenting

Balancing Tech Use and Real-Life Experiences

Chapter 8 63

Educators and AI: Transforming Early Learning Environments

Integrating AI into Early Childhood Education

Professional Development for Educators in AI Integration

Ethical Considerations and Best Practices

"Growing Up Smart: Nurturing Early Childhood in the Age of AI"

Chapter 9 72

Beyond the Classroom: AI and Early Childhood Policy

Policy Implications of AI in Early Childhood

Ensuring Equity and Access in AI-Driven Early Childhood Initiatives

Advocacy and Future Directions

Chapter 10 82

Conclusion: Shaping a Bright Future for Early Childhood in the Age of AI

Reflections on the Intersection of AI and Early Childhood

Key Takeaways and Recommendations

References 90

Chapter 1

An Introduction to the World of Artificial Intelligence

Setting the Stage: Early Childhood and the Emergence of AI

Early childhood is a critical period in human development, shaping the foundation for lifelong learning, behavior, and health (Shonkoff & Phillips, 2000). As technology rapidly evolves, the emergence of artificial intelligence (AI) introduces new dynamics into the early childhood landscape. Artificial intelligence encompasses a range of technologies that simulate human intelligence, including machine learning, natural language processing, and robotics (Russell & Norvig, 2022). These advancements hold promise for enhancing various aspects of early childhood development, from cognitive skills to language acquisition and social interaction (Belpaeme et al., 2018). However, they also raise complex questions and challenges regarding their ethical implications, impact on human relationships, and equitable access (DiSalvo & DiSalvo, 2020). Thus, understanding the intersection of early childhood and AI is essential for educators, policymakers, parents, and researchers to navigate this evolving landscape effectively.

The integration of AI into early childhood settings has the potential to revolutionize learning experiences and outcomes (Papert, 1993). For instance, AI-powered educational apps and games can provide personalized learning experiences tailored to individual children's needs and preferences (VanLehn, 2011). These tools can adapt to a child's learning pace, style, and interests, fostering engagement and motivation (Mitrovic & Ohlsson, 2012). Moreover, AI algorithms can analyze vast amounts of data to identify patterns in children's learning trajectories, enabling educators to make data-driven decisions to support student success (Arroyo & Woolf, 2003). Additionally, AI-powered virtual assistants can offer valuable support to teachers by automating administrative tasks, providing real-time feedback on student performance, and offering personalized recommendations for instructional strategies (Holstein et al., 2020). By leveraging AI technologies effectively, educators can create more inclusive, responsive, and effective learning environments for young children.

However, alongside these opportunities, the integration of AI in early childhood also raises significant ethical considerations and concerns (Floridi & Cowls, 2019). One primary concern is the potential for AI technologies to exacerbate existing inequalities in access to high-quality early childhood education (O'Neill et al., 2020). Children from marginalized communities may face barriers to accessing AI-driven learning tools due to factors such as socioeconomic status, geographic location, or lack of internet connectivity (Warschauer & Matuchniak, 2010). Moreover, there are concerns about data privacy and security, particularly regarding the collection and use of sensitive information about young children (Kahn et al., 2018). As AI algorithms rely on vast datasets to function effectively, there is a risk of perpetuating biases and stereotypes present in the data, leading to unfair or discriminatory outcomes for certain groups of children (Crawford & Paglen, 2019). Additionally, there are ethical questions about the role of AI in shaping children's social and emotional development, as human relationships and interactions are central to healthy child development (García et al., 2021). Thus, it is essential to approach the integration of AI in early childhood with careful consideration of its potential benefits and risks, ensuring that it serves the best interests of all children.

In conclusion, the emergence of AI presents both exciting possibilities and complex challenges for early childhood development. By harnessing the power of AI technologies thoughtfully and ethically, we can enhance learning experiences, support educators, and promote positive outcomes for young children. However, it is crucial to address concerns related to equity, privacy, and the human impact of AI to ensure that all children have access to the opportunities afforded by these advancements. As we navigate this evolving landscape, collaboration among educators, policymakers, researchers, and technology developers will be essential to shape a future where AI enriches rather than detracts from early childhood experiences.

The Significance of Early Childhood Development

Early childhood development is a critical phase that lays the foundation for a child's future health, well-being, and success in life (Shonkoff & Phillips, 2000). This period, spanning from birth to around eight years old, is characterized by rapid growth and development across multiple domains, including physical, cognitive, social, and emotional (National Scientific Council on the Developing Child, 2007). Research has shown that experiences during early childhood shape the architecture of the brain, establishing neural connections that form the basis for learning, behavior, and health throughout life (Center on the Developing Child, 2010). Therefore, understanding the significance of early childhood development is essential for informing policies, programs, and interventions that support children's optimal growth and development.

One of the most critical aspects of early childhood development is brain development. During the first few years of life, the brain undergoes significant growth and development, with billions of neurons forming connections through synapses (Council on Early Childhood et al., 2011). These neural connections are essential for various cognitive functions, including language acquisition, problem-solving, and emotional regulation (Johnson, 2001). Research has shown that early experiences, such as responsive caregiving, stimulating environments, and positive interactions with caregivers, play a crucial role in shaping the developing brain (Shonkoff et al., 2012). Conversely, adverse experiences, such as neglect, abuse, or exposure to toxins, can disrupt healthy brain development and have long-term consequences for children's cognitive and emotional functioning (Anda et al., 2006).

In addition to brain development, early childhood is a critical period for establishing social and emotional skills. During these formative years, children learn to regulate their emotions, understand social cues, and form relationships with others (Denham et al., 2007). These skills lay the foundation for positive social interactions, effective communication, and the ability to navigate complex social situations later in life (Eisenberg et al., 2000). Moreover, research has shown that social and emotional competence in early childhood is associated with various positive outcomes, including academic achievement, mental health, and well-being (Jones et al., 2015). Therefore, interventions that promote social and emotional development in early childhood can have far-reaching benefits for children's overall development and success.

Furthermore, early childhood is a critical period for physical development and health. Proper nutrition, access to healthcare, and safe, nurturing environments are essential for supporting children's physical growth and well-being (Black et al., 2013). Adequate nutrition during early childhood is particularly important, as it supports healthy growth and development and reduces the risk of chronic diseases later in life (Victora et al., 2008). Additionally, early childhood experiences can influence lifelong health behaviors, such as diet, exercise, and substance use (Halfon et al., 2014). Therefore, efforts to promote healthy behaviors and prevent childhood obesity and other health issues must begin early in life to have the greatest impact.

In conclusion, early childhood development is a critical period that lays the foundation for children's future health, well-being, and success. Understanding the significance of early childhood development is essential for informing policies, programs, and interventions that support optimal growth and development during this formative period. By investing in early childhood, we can promote positive outcomes for children, families, and society as a whole.

Chapter 2
Understanding AI Basic

What Is AI?

Artificial Intelligence (AI) refers to the simulation of human intelligence in machines that are programmed to think and learn like humans (Russell & Norvig, 2022). The goal of AI is to create systems that can perform tasks that would typically require human intelligence, such as reasoning, problem-solving, perception, learning, and language understanding. AI technologies encompass a wide range of techniques and approaches, including machine learning, natural language processing, computer vision, robotics, and expert systems. These technologies enable machines to analyze vast amounts of data, recognize patterns, make decisions, and interact with the world in ways that mimic human cognition.

One of the fundamental concepts in AI is machine learning, which involves algorithms that enable machines to learn from data and improve their performance over time without being explicitly programmed (Alpaydin, 2020). Machine learning algorithms use statistical techniques to identify patterns in data and make predictions or decisions based on those patterns. There are various types of machine learning algorithms, including supervised learning, unsupervised learning, and reinforcement learning, each suited to different types of tasks and data.

Supervised learning is one of the most common approaches in machine learning, where the algorithm is trained on labeled data, meaning that the input data is paired with the correct output or target variable (Goodfellow et al., 2016). During training, the algorithm learns to map input data to the correct output by adjusting its internal parameters based on the differences between its predictions and the true labels. Once trained, the algorithm can make predictions on new, unseen data.

Unsupervised learning, on the other hand, involves training algorithms on unlabeled data, where the goal is to discover hidden patterns or structures within the data (Bishop, 2006). These algorithms learn to represent the underlying distribution of the data, such as clustering similar data points together or dimensionality reduction to capture the essential features of the data.

Reinforcement learning is a type of machine learning where algorithms learn to make sequential decisions by interacting with an environment and receiving feedback in the form of rewards or penalties (Sutton & Barto, 2018). The algorithm learns to maximize cumulative rewards over time by exploring different actions and learning from the outcomes of those actions.

In addition to machine learning, AI encompasses other techniques such as natural language processing (NLP), which enables machines to understand and generate human language, and computer vision, which enables machines to interpret and analyze visual information from images or videos (Jurafsky & Martin, 2020). These technologies have numerous applications across various domains, including healthcare, finance, transportation, education, and entertainment.

Furthermore, AI encompasses robotics, which involves the design and development of machines that can perform tasks autonomously or semi-autonomously (Murphy, 2000). Robots equipped with AI capabilities can perceive their environment, make decisions, and execute actions to accomplish tasks such as manufacturing, logistics, exploration, and assistance in healthcare or domestic settings.

While AI has made significant advancements in recent years, it also poses various challenges and considerations, including ethical, societal, and technical issues. Ethical concerns surrounding AI include issues related to bias and fairness in algorithms, privacy and data security, transparency and accountability, and the potential impact on employment and socioeconomic inequality (Floridi & Cowls, 2019). Additionally, there are technical challenges such as the interpretability and explainability of AI systems, robustness and reliability in real-world settings, and scalability and efficiency in handling large-scale data and complex tasks (Goodfellow et al., 2016).

In conclusion, Artificial Intelligence (AI) encompasses a broad range of technologies and approaches aimed at simulating human intelligence in machines. From machine learning to natural language processing, computer vision, and robotics, AI has numerous applications across various domains. While AI has the potential to revolutionize industries and improve human life in many ways, it also raises important ethical, societal, and technical considerations that must be addressed to ensure its responsible development and deployment.

AI's Impact on Society

Artificial Intelligence (AI) has emerged as a transformative force that is reshaping various aspects of society, including industries, economies, governance, and daily life. As AI technologies continue to advance rapidly, their impact on society becomes increasingly profound, presenting both opportunities and challenges. This paper explores the multifaceted impact of AI on society across different domains, examining its implications for healthcare, finance, transportation, education, employment, and governance.

Healthcare is one of the domains profoundly impacted by AI, where its applications range from diagnostics and treatment to personalized medicine and drug discovery. AI-powered diagnostic tools can analyze medical images, detect patterns, and assist healthcare professionals in diagnosing diseases with greater accuracy and efficiency (Esteva et al., 2019). For example, deep learning algorithms have been developed to diagnose skin cancer and diabetic retinopathy with accuracy comparable to human experts (Esteva et al., 2017; Gulshan et al., 2016). Additionally, AI-driven predictive analytics can help forecast disease outbreaks, allocate resources, and personalize treatment plans based on patients' genetic profiles and medical history (Obermeyer & Emanuel, 2016). However, the integration of AI in healthcare raises concerns regarding data privacy, security, and bias in algorithms, as well as the potential impact on healthcare professionals' roles and job displacement (Price et al., 2019).

In finance, AI is revolutionizing how financial institutions operate, from risk assessment and fraud detection to investment management and customer service. AI-powered algorithms analyze vast amounts of financial data, identify market trends, and make real-time trading decisions with speed and accuracy beyond human capabilities (Ghahramani, 2015). Moreover, AI-driven chatbots and virtual assistants provide personalized recommendations, answer customer inquiries, and streamline banking processes, enhancing the customer experience (Budac et al., 2020). However, concerns arise regarding the potential for AI to contribute to financial market volatility, systemic risks, and algorithmic biases that may perpetuate inequalities (Das & Pandey, 2020).

In transportation, AI is driving innovation in autonomous vehicles, intelligent traffic management systems, and predictive maintenance solutions, promising safer, more efficient, and sustainable transportation networks. Autonomous vehicles equipped with AI technologies can navigate complex environments, reduce traffic accidents, and optimize routes to minimize congestion and emissions (Kaplan et al., 2016). Furthermore, AI-powered ride-hailing and logistics platforms optimize resource allocation, improve service reliability, and enhance urban mobility (Xu et al., 2020). However, the widespread deployment of autonomous vehicles raises concerns about safety, liability, regulatory oversight, and the potential displacement of jobs in transportation-related industries (Fagnant &Kockelman, 2015).

In education, AI technologies are transforming teaching and learning, enabling personalized learning experiences, adaptive assessment tools, and intelligent tutoring systems. AI-driven educational platforms analyze students' learning preferences, strengths, and weaknesses to deliver customized content, feedback, and support (Holstein et al., 2020). Moreover, AI-powered virtual assistants and chatbots assist educators in administrative tasks, grading assignments, and providing real-time feedback, freeing up time for personalized instruction and student engagement (Baker et al., 2008). However, concerns arise regarding the potential for AI to perpetuate educational inequalities, data privacy risks, and the need for human oversight and ethical guidelines in AI-driven education (Williamson, 2020).

In employment, AI is reshaping the labor market, automating routine tasks, augmenting human capabilities, and creating new job opportunities. AI-driven technologies such as robotic process automation (RPA), natural language processing (NLP), and machine learning algorithms are transforming industries such as manufacturing, retail, and customer service (Brynjolfsson & McAfee, 2014). While AI has the potential to increase productivity, efficiency, and innovation in the workplace, it also raises concerns about job displacement, skill mismatches, and the need for lifelong learning and reskilling programs to adapt to the changing demands of the digital economy (Acemoglu & Restrepo, 2018).

In governance, AI technologies are being deployed to enhance public services, improve decision-making, and address societal challenges. AI-powered predictive analytics help government agencies forecast and mitigate risks, optimize resource allocation, and enhance emergency response capabilities (Yang & Koenig-Archibugi, 2017). Moreover, AI-driven chatbots and virtual assistants streamline citizen engagement, facilitate access to information and services, and improve transparency and accountability in governance (Hemsley & Mason, 2013). However, concerns arise regarding the ethical use of AI in governance, including issues of bias, fairness, privacy, and accountability, as well as the need for regulatory frameworks and public oversight to ensure responsible AI deployment (Mittelstadt et al., 2016).

In conclusion, Artificial Intelligence (AI) has a profound impact on society across various domains, transforming industries, reshaping labor markets, and raising important ethical, social, and economic considerations. While AI presents opportunities for innovation, efficiency, and human advancement, it also poses challenges related to data privacy, algorithmic bias, job displacement, and societal inequalities. Addressing these challenges requires collaborative efforts among policymakers, technologists, ethicists, and society as a whole to ensure that AI technologies are developed and deployed responsibly, ethically, and equitably.

AI in Education and Child Development

In recent years, the integration of Artificial Intelligence (AI) into education has garnered significant attention as educators seek innovative ways to enhance learning experiences and support child development. From personalized learning platforms to intelligent tutoring systems, AI offers a wide array of tools and technologies that have the potential to revolutionize educational practices. Moreover, as society embraces digital transformation, understanding the implications of AI in education becomes increasingly crucial, particularly in shaping the future of child development in the digital age.

Evolution of AI in Education:

The evolution of AI in education can be traced back to the early development of intelligent tutoring systems (ITS) in the 1970s. These early systems aimed to provide personalized instruction and feedback to students, adapting to their individual learning needs (Koedinger & Corbett, 2006). Over the decades, advancements in AI technologies have led to the emergence of more sophisticated educational tools, including adaptive learning platforms and educational chatbots, which offer personalized support and assistance to learners (Baker et al., 2010).

Applications of AI in Education:

One of the key applications of AI in education is intelligent tutoring systems (ITS), which use AI algorithms to provide individualized instruction and feedback to students. These systems analyze students' learning behaviors and performance data to tailor instruction to their specific needs (Mitrovic & Ohlsson, 1999). Additionally, adaptive learning platforms leverage AI to deliver personalized learning experiences, adjusting the pace and content of instruction based on students' mastery of concepts (Blikstein, 2013). Educational chatbots, powered by AI, provide on-demand support to students, answering questions, providing explanations, and facilitating learning activities (Holstein et al., 2020).

Benefits of AI in Education

The integration of AI in education offers several benefits for learners, educators, and educational institutions. Personalized learning experiences, facilitated by AI technologies, enable students to progress at their own pace and receive targeted support in areas where they struggle (Luckin, 2017). Moreover, AI-driven tools can help educators identify students' learning needs and provide timely interventions to address them, ultimately improving learning outcomes (VanLehn, 2011). Additionally, AI enables educational institutions to collect and analyze vast amounts of data on student performance, facilitating data-driven decision-making and improving instructional practices (Brynjolfsson & McAfee, 2014).

Challenges and Limitations: Despite the potential benefits, the integration of AI in education also poses challenges and limitations. Ethical considerations, such as data privacy and algorithmic bias, raise concerns about the responsible use of AI technologies in educational settings (Anderson, 1983). Moreover, technical barriers, such as the integration of AI systems with existing educational infrastructure and the need for technical expertise among educators, present challenges for widespread adoption (Baker et al., 2010). Additionally, socio-economic factors, including disparities in access to technology and digital literacy skills, may exacerbate inequalities in education (Brynjolfsson & McAfee, 2014).

AI and Child Development: The role of AI in child development extends beyond academic learning to encompass socio-emotional, cognitive, and ethical development. AI-driven educational tools can stimulate critical thinking skills, creativity, and problem-solving abilities in children, providing opportunities for exploration and discovery (Blikstein, 2013). Moreover, AI technologies can support socio-emotional development by fostering empathy, collaboration, and communication skills through interactive learning experiences (Mitrovic & Ohlsson, 1999). Furthermore, AI can play a role in shaping children's ethical and moral development by promoting responsible use of technology and encouraging ethical decision-making (Anderson, 1983).

Future Directions and Implications: Looking ahead, the future of AI in education holds promise for continued innovation and transformation. Advances in AI technologies, such as natural language processing and machine learning, are likely to enable even more sophisticated educational tools and applications (Luckin, 2017). Moreover, as AI becomes more integrated into educational settings, it is essential to consider the broader implications for society, including the ethical, social, and economic implications of AI-driven education (Brynjolfsson & McAfee, 2014). Additionally, policymakers and educators must collaborate to develop frameworks and guidelines for the responsible use of AI in education, ensuring that it benefits all learners and promotes equitable access to quality education (VanLehn, 2011).

Conclusion

In conclusion, the integration of AI into education has the potential to revolutionize teaching, learning, and child development. From personalized learning platforms to intelligent tutoring systems, AI-driven technologies offer innovative solutions to address the diverse needs of learners. Moreover, AI has the potential to support socio-emotional, cognitive, and ethical development in children, providing opportunities for growth and learning. However, the responsible integration of AI in education requires careful consideration of ethical, social, and technical considerations to ensure that it benefits all learners and promotes equitable access to quality education. By harnessing the power of AI, educators can create engaging, personalized learning experiences that empower children to thrive in the digital age.

Chapter 3

The Developing Mind: Early Childhood Cognitive Development

Overview of Cognitive Development in Early Childhood

In the early stages of childhood, cognitive development undergoes remarkable transformations, laying the foundation for a child's lifelong learning journey. This narrative delves into the overview of cognitive development during early childhood, highlighting key theories, milestones, and factors that influence this crucial period of growth.

Piaget's theory of cognitive development provides a foundational framework for understanding how children construct knowledge and make sense of their world. According to Piaget, cognitive development progresses through distinct stages, including the sensorimotor stage (birth to 2 years), the preoperational stage (2 to 7 years), the concrete operational stage (7 to 11 years), and the formal operational stage (11 years and older). During the sensorimotor stage, infants explore their environment through sensory experiences and develop object permanence—the understanding that objects continue to exist even when they are out of sight (Piaget, 1954). As children transition to the preoperational stage, they begin to use language and symbols to represent objects and engage in imaginative play. However, they exhibit egocentrism—the inability to see things from others' perspectives—and struggle with conservation—the understanding that quantity remains the same despite changes in appearance.

Vygotsky's sociocultural theory emphasizes the role of social interaction and cultural context in cognitive development. According to Vygotsky, children learn through social interactions with more knowledgeable others, such as parents, teachers, and peers, who provide scaffolding—support and guidance—to facilitate learning (Vygotsky, 1978). The concept of the zone of proximal development (ZPD) refers to the difference between what a child can do independently and what they can achieve with assistance. By engaging in collaborative activities and receiving guidance from others, children can advance their cognitive skills and problem-solving abilities.

In addition to theoretical frameworks, understanding the key milestones of cognitive development in early childhood is essential. During the preschool years, children demonstrate significant advancements in language development, memory, and problem-solving skills. They begin to ask questions, engage in symbolic play, and show curiosity about the world around them. Piagetian tasks, such as conservation tasks and classification tasks, provide insights into children's cognitive abilities and understanding of concepts such as number, quantity, and identity.

Factors such as genetics, environment, and experiences shape cognitive development during early childhood. Genetic predispositions influence cognitive abilities and learning styles, while environmental factors, such as socioeconomic status, access to education, and family dynamics, play a crucial role in providing opportunities for learning and intellectual stimulation (Bronfenbrenner, 1979). Enriched environments that offer exposure to a variety of stimuli, activities, and social interactions promote cognitive growth and skill development.

Moreover, recent research highlights the role of early childhood education and interventions in fostering cognitive development. High-quality early childhood programs, such as preschools and daycare centers, provide structured learning experiences and socialization opportunities that support cognitive, social, and emotional development (Barnett et al., 2008). Evidence-based interventions, such as early literacy programs and cognitive enrichment activities, have been shown to enhance cognitive skills, school readiness, and academic achievement in young children (Heckman et al., 2010).

In conclusion, cognitive development during early childhood is a dynamic and multifaceted process influenced by genetic, environmental, and experiential factors. Theories such as Piaget's theory and Vygotsky's sociocultural theory offer valuable insights into the mechanisms underlying cognitive growth and learning. Understanding the key milestones and factors that shape cognitive development in early childhood is essential for parents, educators, and policymakers to support children's learning and overall well-being.

How AI Influences Cognitive Skills

Artificial Intelligence (AI) exerts a significant influence on cognitive skills, impacting various aspects of learning, problem-solving, and decision-making. Here's an exploration of how AI influences cognitive skills:

Cognitive Evolution: The AI Influence

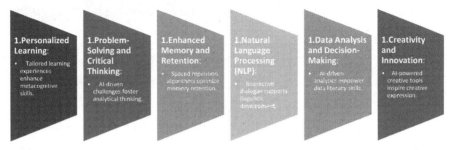

Figure 1

Personalized Learning: AI-powered educational platforms utilize algorithms to adapt learning experiences based on individual learner's needs, preferences, and performance. By analyzing data on learner's interactions, AI can tailor content, pacing, and feedback to optimize learning outcomes. This personalized approach fosters metacognitive skills, such as self-regulation and reflection, as learners take ownership of their learning process.

Problem-Solving and Critical Thinking: AI technologies, such as intelligent tutoring systems and educational games, present learners with complex problems and challenges that require analytical thinking, reasoning, and creativity to solve. By engaging with AI-driven simulations and scenarios, learners develop problem-solving strategies, evaluate multiple solutions, and make informed decisions—a process that enhances cognitive flexibility and critical thinking skills.

Enhanced Memory and Retention: AI-powered adaptive learning systems employ spaced repetition algorithms to optimize the timing and frequency of learning interventions, facilitating long-term memory retention. By strategically reviewing and reinforcing learning materials at optimal intervals, AI helps learners encode information more effectively, strengthen neural connections, and retain knowledge over time—a process that supports cognitive skills related to memory and recall.

Natural Language Processing (NLP): NLP technologies enable AI systems to understand, process, and generate human language, facilitating interactive dialogue and communication between learners and virtual tutors or chatbots. Through conversational interactions, learners engage in language-rich environments that promote linguistic development, vocabulary acquisition, and comprehension skills. Additionally, NLP-driven language learning applications offer opportunities for language practice, feedback, and immersion, enhancing linguistic fluency and communication proficiency.

Data Analysis and Decision-Making: AI-driven analytics tools provide educators and learners with insights into learning progress, performance trends, and areas for improvement. By analyzing vast amounts of data generated from learner interactions, AI identifies patterns, trends, and correlations that inform instructional strategies, intervention plans, and learning pathways. Learners develop data literacy skills as they interpret visualizations, draw conclusions, and make evidence-based decisions—a process that enhances cognitive skills related to data analysis and inference.

Creativity and Innovation: AI technologies, such as generative algorithms and creative assistants, inspire and facilitate creative expression by generating novel ideas, designs, and solutions. Through collaboration with AI-driven creative tools, learners explore new possibilities, experiment with different approaches, and iterate on their creations—a process that fosters creativity, imagination, and innovation. Additionally, AI-powered content creation tools enable learners to produce multimedia artifacts, such as artworks, music compositions, and storytelling, expanding their creative repertoire and expression.

In summary, AI influences cognitive skills by providing personalized learning experiences, promoting problem-solving and critical thinking, enhancing memory and retention, facilitating language development, empowering data analysis and decision-making, and fostering creativity and innovation. As AI continues to evolve and integrate into educational contexts, it holds the potential to enhance cognitive development, empower learners, and shape the future of education.

AI-Assisted Learning Tools for Cognitive Development

Artificial Intelligence (AI) has revolutionized education by offering sophisticated tools that augment cognitive development in learners. These AI-assisted learning tools leverage advanced algorithms to personalize learning experiences, cater to individual needs, and optimize cognitive growth (Somyürek& Atasoy, 2020). Personalized learning, facilitated by AI, adapts content and pacing according to learners' preferences and performance levels, fostering metacognitive skills such as self-regulation and reflection (Kolb, 2021). Through the analysis of vast amounts of learner data, AI can identify learning patterns and tailor interventions to enhance cognitive processes like problem-solving and critical thinking (Sinha et al., 2019).

One significant contribution of AI-assisted learning tools is the optimization of memory retention through spaced repetition algorithms (Kostopoulos et al., 2020). These algorithms strategically reinforce learning materials at optimal intervals, facilitating effective encoding and retention of information in long-term memory (Kaufman & Khosravi, 2021). Moreover, AI-driven natural language processing (NLP) technologies enable interactive communication between learners and virtual tutors or chatbots, enhancing linguistic development and comprehension skills (AlZoubi et al., 2022). Learners engage in language-rich environments, practicing communication and receiving immediate feedback, which aids in language acquisition and fluency (Zhang & Guan, 2020).

Furthermore, AI-driven analytics tools provide educators and learners with valuable insights into learning progress and performance trends, supporting data-driven decision-making (Mohamed et al., 2021). By analyzing learner interactions and performance data, AI identifies areas for improvement and suggests personalized learning pathways, enhancing cognitive skills related to data analysis and inference (Feng et al., 2021). Additionally, AI technologies inspire creativity and innovation by generating novel ideas and facilitating experimentation with different approaches (Karumbaiah et al., 2020). Learners collaborate with AI-powered creative assistants to produce multimedia artifacts, fostering imaginative thinking and innovative problem-solving (Tang et al., 2021).

In summary, AI-assisted learning tools play a crucial role in cognitive development by offering personalized learning experiences, optimizing memory retention, enhancing language skills, facilitating data-driven decision-making, and fostering creativity and innovation. These tools hold immense potential to revolutionize education, catering to diverse learning needs and empowering learners to thrive in the rapidly evolving digital age.

Chapter 4
Social and Emotional Development in the Digital Age

Importance of Social and Emotional Skills in Early Childhood

In the early years of a child's life, the building blocks of social and emotional skills are laid down, setting the stage for their future development. According to the Center on the Developing Child at Harvard University, these skills encompass a child's ability to form secure attachments, regulate emotions, and interact effectively with others (Center on the Developing Child, 2007). From infancy, caregivers play a crucial role in nurturing these skills through responsive interactions and emotional support.

As children grow, their social and emotional competencies become increasingly important for navigating the complexities of relationships and social interactions. Strong social skills enable children to build positive connections with peers and adults, fostering empathy and cooperation. Research conducted by Denham and her colleagues underscores the role of emotional competence in promoting healthy social interactions and reducing behavioral problems (Denham et al., 2003).

Beyond interpersonal relationships, social and emotional skills have far-reaching implications for academic achievement and overall well-being. Studies have shown that children with higher levels of social competence in kindergarten tend to perform better academically and have higher rates of high school graduation (Jones et al., 2015). Additionally, the ability to regulate emotions and behavior is essential for school readiness, enabling children to focus attention, follow instructions, and persist in challenging tasks (Raver et al., 2011).

Moreover, social and emotional skills contribute to resilience, helping children cope with stress and adversity. Positive relationships and emotional regulation play a key role in mitigating the effects of adverse experiences on children's well-being. Learning conflict resolution and problem-solving skills in early childhood equips children with the tools to navigate conflicts peacefully and build constructive relationships (Jones & Bouffard, 2012).

Parents, caregivers, schools, and communities all play a vital role in nurturing children's social and emotional development. Attachment theory highlights the significance of responsive caregiving and secure attachments in promoting emotional security and social competence (Bowlby, 1982). Supportive environments in schools and communities, along with the implementation of social-emotional learning programs, further reinforce these skills and promote positive social behaviors (Zins et al., 2004).

Investing in social and emotional development in early childhood yields long-term benefits for individuals and society as a whole. Nobel laureate James Heckman's research emphasizes the economic and social returns of early childhood interventions that promote social and emotional skills, including higher educational attainment, better employment outcomes, and reduced rates of crime and incarceration (Heckman, 2006).

In essence, the journey of social and emotional development in early childhood is foundational, shaping children's abilities to navigate relationships, regulate emotions, and thrive in various aspects of life. Through nurturing environments and supportive relationships, children can develop the essential skills needed for success and well-being in the years to come.

Challenges and Opportunities of AI in Social and Emotional Learning

Integrating Artificial Intelligence (AI) into Social and Emotional Learning (SEL) initiatives presents both challenges and opportunities in educational settings. One significant challenge lies in the ethical considerations surrounding AI implementation. As Biklen and Pangrazio (2019) discuss, there is a risk of AI algorithms perpetuating biases or reinforcing stereotypes, particularly in areas related to emotion recognition and behavioral analysis. Moreover, the dependency on AI technologies may diminish the role of human educators and interpersonal relationships, potentially hindering students' social and emotional development (Biklen & Pangrazio, 2019). Alongside ethical concerns, ensuring data privacy and security poses another challenge. With AI-driven SEL platforms collecting vast amounts of sensitive data on students' emotions and behaviors, safeguarding this information from breaches and unauthorized access is paramount (Cen, 2020).

However, amidst these challenges lie numerous opportunities for leveraging AI to enhance SEL outcomes. One such opportunity is the potential for personalized learning experiences. Pangrazio et al. (2020) highlight how AI-powered SEL platforms can adapt content and interventions to meet individual students' needs, preferences, and learning styles. By providing personalized feedback and recommendations, AI enables students to engage in self-directed learning and develop self-awareness and self-regulation skills (Pangrazio et al., 2020). Additionally, AI algorithms offer early intervention and support by identifying signs of emotional distress or behavioral issues in students. Sani et al. (2021) discuss how AI-driven analytics tools can facilitate early detection of mental health concerns and enable educators to intervene proactively, promoting timely support strategies.

Furthermore, AI-driven analytics tools offer valuable insights into students' social and emotional development, performance trends, and areas for improvement (Pangrazio et al., 2020). By analyzing vast amounts of data, AI identifies patterns and correlations that inform instructional strategies and intervention plans, empowering educators to make evidence-based decisions (Pangrazio et al., 2020). Moreover, AI technologies have the potential to make SEL resources more accessible and inclusive for diverse learners. Tasdemir and Kitsantas (2020) discuss how adaptive learning features and customizable interfaces in AI-driven SEL platforms cater to individual learning needs, promoting equitable access to educational opportunities.

In conclusion, while challenges such as ethical considerations and data privacy concerns must be addressed, the opportunities afforded by integrating AI into SEL initiatives are substantial. By leveraging AI responsibly, educators can enhance personalized learning experiences, provide early intervention and support, gain valuable insights into students' social and emotional development, and promote inclusivity in educational settings.

Balancing Screen Time and Human Interaction

Finding a balance between screen time and human interaction is a significant concern in the digital age, particularly in educational contexts. As technology becomes increasingly integrated into classrooms, educators and parents alike grapple with how to optimize the use of digital tools while preserving opportunities for face-to-face interaction and social-emotional learning (SEL). Research suggests that excessive screen time can have detrimental effects on children's social development and well-being (Twenge & Campbell, 2018). Excessive use of screens, particularly for passive activities such as watching videos or playing games, may limit opportunities for real-world interactions and hinder the development of crucial social skills (Twenge & Campbell, 2018). Furthermore, excessive screen time has been associated with negative health outcomes, including increased sedentary behavior, sleep disturbances, and decreased physical activity (Hale & Guan, 2015). Thus, there is a growing recognition of the importance of balancing screen time with opportunities for meaningful human interaction.

However, it is essential to recognize that technology can also facilitate positive social interactions and enhance learning experiences when used judiciously. Digital tools, such as video conferencing platforms and social media, enable individuals to connect with others regardless of physical distance, fostering social connections and collaboration (Hampton et al., 2015). In educational settings, technology can provide opportunities for students to engage in collaborative learning activities, communicate with peers and experts, and access educational resources beyond the confines of the classroom (Hampton et al., 2015). Additionally, digital platforms can support social-emotional learning (SEL) by providing students with opportunities to develop empathy, communication skills, and digital citizenship (Greenhow et al., 2019). For example, online platforms may facilitate discussions about diverse perspectives, encourage active listening, and promote responsible online behavior.

To strike a balance between screen time and human interaction, educators and parents must adopt a mindful approach to technology integration. This involves setting clear boundaries and guidelines for screen use, emphasizing the importance of face-to-face interactions, and promoting activities that foster social-emotional development (Greenfield et al., 2015). For instance, educators can design learning experiences that incorporate both digital and offline activities, allowing students to leverage technology while also engaging in hands-on, collaborative tasks (Greenfield et al., 2015). Likewise, parents can model healthy screen habits, prioritize quality family time without screens, and encourage outdoor play and face-to-face interactions with peers (Twenge & Campbell, 2018).

In conclusion, finding a balance between screen time and human interaction is essential for promoting children's social development, well-being, and academic success. While technology offers numerous benefits in educational settings, it is crucial to approach its use mindfully and thoughtfully. By prioritizing opportunities for face-to-face interactions, setting clear boundaries for screen use, and integrating technology in ways that support social-emotional learning, educators and parents can help children navigate the digital world while fostering healthy social relationships and emotional growth.

Chapter 5
Language Acquisition and AI

Language Development Milestones in Early Childhood

Language development milestones in early childhood mark crucial stages in a child's linguistic journey, reflecting their progress in acquiring and mastering language skills. According to the American Speech-Language-Hearing Association (ASHA), these milestones encompass various aspects of language, including vocabulary acquisition, grammar, and communication skills (ASHA, n.d.). During the first year of life, infants typically demonstrate foundational language abilities, such as cooing and babbling, which lay the groundwork for later language development (ASHA, n.d.). By around 12 months of age, most children utter their first words, signaling the onset of expressive language and the ability to communicate basic needs and desires (ASHA, n.d.).

As children progress through early childhood, their language skills become more sophisticated, encompassing an expanding vocabulary and increasing complexity in grammar and sentence structure. By the age of two, children typically begin combining words to form simple sentences, demonstrating an understanding of basic grammar rules and language conventions (ASHA, n.d.). This stage, often referred to as the "two-word stage," marks a significant milestone in language development, as children transition from single-word utterances to more complex forms of communication (ASHA, n.d.).

Between the ages of three and five, children undergo rapid language development, acquiring a broader vocabulary and demonstrating greater fluency in speech. According to the Centers for Disease Control and Prevention (CDC), by the age of three, children typically use approximately 200 to 1,000 words and can engage in more extended conversations with adults and peers (CDC, 2020). Additionally, children at this age begin to grasp more complex grammatical structures, such as plurals, possessives, and verb tenses, further enhancing their expressive and receptive language skills (CDC, 2020).

By the time children reach kindergarten age, typically around five years old, they have developed a solid foundation in language and communication skills. At this stage, children can express themselves clearly and effectively, engage in conversations on a wide range of topics, and understand and follow increasingly complex instructions (ASHA, n.d.). Moreover, children demonstrate a growing awareness of language and its use in different contexts, such as storytelling, role-playing, and problem-solving (ASHA, n.d.).

Throughout early childhood, language development is influenced by various factors, including genetics, environment, and social interactions. According to research published in the Journal of Child Language, children's language development is shaped by their interactions with caregivers and exposure to language-rich environments (Rowe, 2012). Positive, responsive interactions with caregivers, exposure to diverse language models, and opportunities for meaningful communication play a crucial role in supporting children's language development (Rowe, 2012).

In conclusion, language development milestones in early childhood reflect children's progression in acquiring and refining language skills. From their first words to more complex forms of communication, children demonstrate remarkable growth in language abilities during the early years of life. By understanding these milestones and providing supportive environments for language learning, caregivers and educators can help foster children's linguistic development and set the stage for future academic success.

AI's Role in Language Learning

Artificial Intelligence (AI) is revolutionizing language learning by offering innovative tools and platforms that cater to individual learners' needs and preferences. One significant role of AI in language learning is personalized instruction. AI-powered language learning platforms utilize algorithms to analyze learners' strengths, weaknesses, and learning styles, allowing for tailored content delivery and adaptive learning experiences (Fang et al., 2018). By providing personalized instruction, AI enables learners to progress at their own pace, focus on areas of difficulty, and receive targeted feedback, thereby enhancing their language acquisition process.

Furthermore, AI facilitates immersive language learning experiences through interactive simulations and virtual environments. Platforms like language learning apps and chatbots leverage Natural Language Processing (NLP) algorithms to engage learners in conversational interactions, providing opportunities for language practice and real-time feedback (Han et al., 2020). Through simulated dialogues and scenarios, learners can develop their language skills in authentic contexts, improving their communication abilities and confidence.

Moreover, AI-driven language learning tools support multimodal learning approaches, incorporating various media formats such as text, audio, video, and images to cater to diverse learning preferences (Chen et al., 2018). For instance, language learning apps may offer interactive exercises, audiovisual content, and gamified activities to engage learners and reinforce language concepts (Chen et al., 2018). By providing multimedia resources, AI enhances learners' engagement and comprehension, facilitating a more interactive and dynamic learning experience.

In addition to personalized instruction and immersive experiences, AI empowers language learners through data-driven insights and analytics. Language learning platforms collect and analyze vast amounts of learner data, including performance metrics, interaction patterns, and learning preferences (Huang et al., 2020). By leveraging data analytics, AI identifies learning trends, evaluates instructional effectiveness, and generates actionable insights for educators and learners (Huang et al., 2020). This data-driven approach enables educators to make informed decisions, optimize instructional strategies, and tailor interventions to meet learners' needs effectively.

Furthermore, AI enhances language learning opportunities by breaking down barriers to access and promoting inclusivity. Language learning platforms powered by AI offer anytime, anywhere access to educational resources, allowing learners to engage in language learning activities at their convenience (Nikolov et al., 2021). Additionally, AI-driven translation tools facilitate cross-cultural communication and collaboration by bridging language barriers and enabling real-time language interpretation (Nikolov et al., 2021). By promoting access and inclusivity, AI expands language learning opportunities for learners worldwide, regardless of geographical location or linguistic background.

Furthermore, AI-driven language assessment tools offer objective and standardized evaluations of learners' language proficiency levels (Kampylis et al., 2020). By analyzing linguistic performance and language usage patterns, AI algorithms generate detailed assessments of learners' speaking, listening, reading, and writing skills (Kampylis et al., 2020). These assessments provide valuable feedback to learners, educators, and institutions, informing instructional decisions, tracking progress, and identifying areas for improvement effectively.

Moreover, AI supports collaborative language learning experiences by facilitating communication and collaboration among learners and educators (Han et al., 2020). Language learning platforms equipped with AI-driven communication tools enable learners to engage in peer-to-peer interactions, group discussions, and collaborative projects (Han et al., 2020). Through collaborative learning experiences, learners can exchange ideas, receive peer feedback, and enhance their language skills through social interaction and collaboration.

In summary, AI plays a transformative role in language learning by offering personalized instruction, immersive experiences, multimodal learning resources, data-driven insights, inclusive access, objective assessments, and collaborative learning opportunities. By harnessing the power of AI, educators and learners can optimize language learning experiences, enhance learning outcomes, and foster a more inclusive and engaging learning environment.

Ethics and Concerns in Language Acquisition with AI

Ethics and concerns in language acquisition with Artificial Intelligence (AI) are paramount as AI-driven language learning tools become increasingly prevalent in educational settings. One significant ethical consideration is the potential reinforcement of biases and stereotypes in AI-generated content and language models. Research has shown that AI algorithms trained on biased datasets may perpetuate stereotypes and discriminatory language patterns, posing risks to learners' linguistic development and social perceptions (Zhao et al., 2017). Furthermore, the use of AI in language acquisition raises concerns about data privacy and security. Language learning platforms collect vast amounts of sensitive learner data, including linguistic proficiency levels, cultural backgrounds, and learning preferences. Ensuring the confidentiality and protection of this data is essential to prevent unauthorized access or misuse (Wang et al., 2020).

Additionally, there are ethical concerns regarding the use of AI-driven language assessment tools in educational settings. AI algorithms used for language assessment may lack transparency and accountability, making it difficult to understand how assessment decisions are made and challenging to challenge results (Hu et al., 2020). Furthermore, AI-generated assessments may not accurately capture the complexity and nuances of language proficiency, leading to potential misinterpretations or misalignments with learners' abilities (Hu et al., 2020). Moreover, there are ethical considerations surrounding the equitable access to AI-driven language learning resources. Language learning platforms equipped with AI technologies may require access to high-speed internet, digital devices, and technical support, which may exacerbate existing inequalities in access to education (Nelson et al., 2017).

Another ethical concern is the potential dehumanization of language learning experiences due to excessive reliance on AI-driven tools and automation. Language learning is inherently a social and interactive process, involving meaningful interactions with peers and educators. Over-reliance on AI technologies may diminish opportunities for authentic communication and interpersonal connections, undermining the development of social and emotional skills in language learners (Skeels et al., 2019). Additionally, there are ethical considerations regarding the accountability and responsibility of AI developers and educators in addressing the ethical implications of AI in language acquisition. Developers and educators must prioritize ethical considerations in the design, implementation, and evaluation of AI-driven language learning tools, ensuring that these technologies promote equity, diversity, and inclusion in educational settings (Wang et al., 2020).

Furthermore, there are ethical concerns regarding the potential commodification and commercialization of language learning with AI. Language learning platforms powered by AI may prioritize profit-driven objectives over educational outcomes, leading to the prioritization of marketable features and content rather than pedagogically sound instructional practices (Nelson et al., 2017). Additionally, there are ethical considerations surrounding the accuracy and reliability of AI-generated content and translations. AI-driven language models may produce erroneous or culturally insensitive translations, leading to misunderstandings or misinterpretations of language and cultural nuances (Zhao et al., 2017).

In conclusion, ethics and concerns in language acquisition with AI encompass a range of complex issues, including biases in AI-generated content, data privacy and security, transparency in language assessment, equitable access to AI-driven resources, dehumanization of language learning experiences, accountability of AI developers and educators, commodification of language learning, and accuracy of AI-generated content. Addressing these ethical considerations requires a concerted effort from stakeholders in education, including policymakers, educators, AI developers, and learners, to ensure that AI technologies are ethically designed, implemented, and evaluated in language acquisition contexts.

Chapter 6
Play, Creativity, and AI

The Vital Role of Play in Early Childhood

Play is universally recognized as a fundamental aspect of early childhood development, contributing significantly to children's physical, cognitive, social, and emotional well-being. As noted by Piaget (1962), play serves as a vehicle for young children to explore, experiment, and make sense of the world around them. Through play, children engage in imaginative and creative activities that promote cognitive skills such as problem-solving, critical thinking, and decision-making (Lillard et al., 2013). Moreover, play fosters the development of language and communication skills, as children engage in symbolic play, storytelling, and social interactions with peers (Lillard et al., 2013).

Furthermore, play plays a vital role in promoting social-emotional development during early childhood. According to Vygotsky (1978), play serves as a zone of proximal development, enabling children to practice social skills, regulate emotions, and develop empathy and perspective-taking abilities. Through cooperative play and pretend play scenarios, children learn to negotiate, take turns, and collaborate with others, laying the foundation for positive social relationships and interpersonal skills (Russ, 2004). Additionally, play provides opportunities for children to express and manage their emotions in a safe and supportive environment, fostering resilience and emotional well-being (Russ, 2004).

Moreover, play contributes to the physical development of young children by promoting gross motor skills, fine motor skills, and spatial awareness. Activities such as running, jumping, climbing, and balancing help children develop strength, coordination, and balance (Pellegrini & Smith, 1998). Furthermore, sensory play experiences, such as exploring textures, shapes, and sounds, stimulate children's senses and enhance their perceptual-motor abilities (Pellegrini & Smith, 1998). By engaging in active and hands-on play experiences, children develop fundamental movement skills that are essential for their overall physical health and well-being.

In addition to its developmental benefits, play has been recognized as a protective factor against stress and adversity in early childhood. According to Ginsburg (2007), play serves as a natural mechanism for stress reduction and relaxation, allowing children to release tension and recharge their emotional resources. Through playful activities, children learn to cope with challenges, regulate their emotions, and build resilience in the face of adversity (Ginsburg, 2007). Moreover, play provides opportunities for children to explore and make sense of their experiences, helping them develop a sense of mastery and control over their environment (Ginsburg, 2007).

Furthermore, play promotes creativity and imagination, fostering innovation, and problem-solving skills in young children. According to Bodrova and Leong (2005), play-based learning experiences stimulate children's curiosity, exploration, and experimentation, leading to novel discoveries and insights. Through open-ended play activities, children engage in divergent thinking, generate multiple solutions to problems, and explore new possibilities

(Bodrova & Leong, 2005). Additionally, pretend play experiences allow children to take on different roles and perspectives, encouraging flexible thinking and imaginative expression (Bodrova & Leong, 2005).

Moreover, play has been shown to positively impact academic achievement and school readiness in early childhood. Research indicates that children who engage in high-quality play experiences during the preschool years demonstrate better literacy, numeracy, and executive function skills later in life (Bodrova & Leong, 2007). Play-based learning approaches, such as Montessori and Reggio Emilia, emphasize hands-on, experiential learning activities that promote inquiry, exploration, and discovery (Bodrova & Leong, 2007). By integrating play into early childhood education, educators can create rich and meaningful learning environments that foster children's intellectual growth and academic success.

In summary, play plays a vital role in early childhood development, contributing to children's physical, cognitive, social, and emotional well-being. Through play, children engage in imaginative, creative, and exploratory activities that promote learning, socialization, and self-expression. By recognizing the importance of play and providing opportunities for playful experiences, educators and caregivers can support children's holistic development and lay the foundation for lifelong learning and success.

AI and Creative Play

Artificial Intelligence (AI) has begun to intersect with creative play, transforming traditional play experiences and offering innovative opportunities for children's engagement and learning. One significant application of AI in creative play is the development of interactive toys and games that utilize AI algorithms to enhance play experiences (Shin et al., 2017). These AI-powered toys can engage children in dynamic and personalized interactions, adapting to their preferences, abilities, and learning goals (Shin et al., 2017). By incorporating AI technologies, toys and games can offer immersive and engaging play experiences that stimulate creativity, imagination, and problem-solving skills in children.

Furthermore, AI-driven creative tools enable children to explore and experiment with various forms of artistic expression, such as music composition, digital art, and storytelling (Togelius et al., 2018). For example, AI-powered music composition tools allow children to create original music compositions by manipulating musical parameters and generating melodies, harmonies, and rhythms (Togelius et al., 2018). Similarly, AI-driven storytelling platforms offer interactive storytelling experiences, where children can co-create narratives with AI-generated characters and scenarios (Togelius et al., 2018). These AI-enabled creative tools empower children to express themselves artistically, experiment with different ideas, and develop their creative potential.

Moreover, AI technologies facilitate collaborative play experiences, where children can engage in cooperative problem-solving activities and creative projects with AI-driven virtual agents or robotic companions (Belpaeme et al., 2018). For instance, AI-powered robots equipped with natural language processing capabilities can interact with children in real-time, offering assistance, feedback, and encouragement during collaborative tasks (Belpaeme et al., 2018). Through collaborative play with AI-driven companions, children can develop teamwork skills, communication skills, and social-emotional competencies, fostering positive relationships and peer interactions.

Additionally, AI-driven storytelling applications offer opportunities for children to engage in imaginative play and role-playing activities, where they can immerse themselves in virtual worlds and fictional scenarios (Shin et al., 2017). These interactive storytelling experiences allow children to assume different roles, explore new identities, and create their narratives, fostering creativity, empathy, and perspective-taking abilities (Shin et al., 2017). By integrating AI technologies into storytelling and imaginative play, educators and caregivers can enhance children's narrative skills, language development, and socio-emotional learning.

Furthermore, AI-powered toys and games can facilitate personalized learning experiences, where children can engage in play-based activities that are tailored to their individual interests, abilities, and learning styles (Togelius et al., 2018). AI algorithms analyze children's interactions and behaviors, providing adaptive feedback, scaffolding, and challenges to support their cognitive development and skill acquisition (Togelius et al., 2018). Through personalized play experiences, children can explore new concepts, solve problems, and learn at their own pace, promoting autonomy, motivation, and engagement in learning.

In conclusion, AI has the potential to revolutionize creative play by offering interactive toys, creative tools, collaborative companions, storytelling applications, and personalized learning experiences that stimulate children's imagination, creativity, and social-emotional development. By integrating AI technologies into play environments, educators and caregivers can create rich and dynamic play experiences that foster children's holistic development and prepare them for success in the digital age.

Fostering Creativity in a Digital World

Fostering creativity in a digital world presents both challenges and opportunities for educators and parents alike. While digital technologies offer unprecedented access to information and tools for creative expression, they also raise concerns about screen time, passive consumption, and the potential homogenization of creative experiences. One key consideration is striking a balance between digital and non-digital creative activities, ensuring that children have opportunities to engage in hands-on, tactile experiences that stimulate their senses and imagination (Livingstone et al., 2017). By integrating both digital and traditional forms of creative expression, educators and parents can create rich and diverse learning environments that cater to children's individual interests and preferences.

Moreover, digital technologies can serve as powerful tools for enhancing creativity and innovation in children. For example, coding and programming platforms offer opportunities for children to learn computational thinking, problem-solving skills, and algorithmic logic through interactive and engaging activities (Resnick et al., 2009). By experimenting with coding, children can design and create their digital projects, such as animations, games, and interactive stories, fostering creativity, experimentation, and self-expression (Resnick et al., 2009).

Additionally, digital platforms provide access to a wealth of creative resources and communities that can inspire and support children's creative endeavors. Online forums, social media platforms, and digital repositories offer opportunities for children to share their work, receive feedback, and collaborate with peers and mentors from around the world (Ito et al., 2010). By participating in online communities and networks, children can gain exposure to diverse perspectives, ideas, and cultural influences, enriching their creative experiences and expanding their creative horizons (Ito et al., 2010).

Furthermore, digital technologies enable children to engage in multimedia storytelling, where they can combine text, images, audio, and video to create immersive and interactive narratives (Peppler et al., 2010). Digital storytelling platforms offer tools and templates that simplify the process of story creation, allowing children to focus on storytelling techniques, character development, and plot structure (Peppler et al., 2010). By experimenting with digital storytelling, children can develop their narrative skills, communication skills, and digital literacy, empowering them to express themselves creatively in the digital age.

Despite the potential benefits of digital technologies for fostering creativity, it is essential to recognize and address the challenges and risks associated with their use. One concern is the passive consumption of digital content, where children spend more time consuming media than actively creating or engaging in creative activities (Livingstone et al., 2017). Excessive screen time and passive consumption of digital media may limit children's opportunities for hands-on exploration, experimentation, and imaginative play, hindering their creative development (Livingstone et al., 2017).

Moreover, there are concerns about the commercialization and commodification of creativity in the digital age. Many digital platforms and products are designed to monetize children's creative activities, promoting consumerism and brand loyalty over artistic expression and experimentation (Ito et al., 2010). Additionally, the gamification of creativity, where children are rewarded for completing tasks or achieving goals, may undermine intrinsic motivation and curiosity, stifling their creativity and autonomy (Resnick et al., 2009).

Furthermore, there are ethical considerations surrounding children's privacy and safety in digital creative spaces. Online platforms and social media networks collect vast amounts of personal data from children, including their preferences, behaviors, and interactions (Ito et al., 2010). Ensuring the privacy and security of children's data is essential to protect their rights and well-being in digital environments (Livingstone et al., 2017). Moreover, educators and parents must educate children about digital citizenship, responsible online behavior, and critical media literacy to empower them to navigate digital spaces safely and ethically (Peppler et al., 2010).

In conclusion, fostering creativity in a digital world requires a balanced approach that leverages the affordances of digital technologies while addressing the challenges and risks associated with their use. By integrating digital and non-digital creative activities, providing opportunities for hands-on exploration and experimentation, and promoting critical media literacy and digital citizenship, educators and parents can empower children to harness the transformative potential of digital technologies for creative expression and innovation.

Chapter 7
Parenting in the AI Era

Parental Guidance in a Digital Age

Parental guidance in a digital age is essential for supporting children's healthy development and well-being in an increasingly connected and technology-driven world. As children spend more time online and engage with digital devices from a young age, parents play a crucial role in helping them navigate the opportunities and challenges of the digital landscape (Livingstone et al., 2017). One key aspect of parental guidance is setting clear boundaries and rules around screen time and digital use, ensuring that children have a healthy balance between online and offline activities (Livingstone et al., 2017). By establishing age-appropriate guidelines for screen time limits, device usage, and online activities, parents can promote healthy habits and reduce the risks of excessive screen time and digital dependence.

Moreover, parental guidance involves actively monitoring and supervising children's online activities, including the websites they visit, the apps they use, and the content they consume (Livingstone et al., 2017). By staying informed about children's digital interactions and experiences, parents can identify potential risks, such as exposure to inappropriate content, cyberbullying, or online predators, and take proactive measures to protect their children's safety and well-being (Livingstone et al., 2017). Additionally, parents can engage in open and ongoing conversations with their children about online safety, privacy, and responsible digital citizenship, empowering them to make informed decisions and navigate digital spaces safely and ethically (Livingstone et al., 2017).

Furthermore, parental guidance involves modeling positive digital behaviors and attitudes for children, serving as role models for responsible and mindful technology use (Livingstone et al., 2017). By demonstrating healthy screen habits, such as limiting screen time, prioritizing face-to-face interactions, and practicing digital etiquette, parents can instill valuable values and norms that guide children's digital behavior and attitudes (Livingstone et al., 2017). Additionally, parents can actively participate in their children's digital lives, engaging in shared activities, such as playing online games, creating digital art, or watching educational videos together, to foster bonding, communication, and collaborative learning experiences (Livingstone et al., 2017).

Moreover, parental guidance encompasses supporting children's digital literacy and critical thinking skills, equipping them with the knowledge, skills, and attitudes needed to navigate and evaluate digital information effectively (Livingstone et al., 2017). By providing guidance on how to assess the credibility, reliability, and relevance of online content, parents can help children develop media literacy and discernment, empowering them to make informed decisions and avoid misinformation, fake news, and online scams (Livingstone et al., 2017). Additionally, parents can encourage children to question, analyze, and reflect critically on the digital media they encounter, fostering a healthy skepticism and curiosity that enhances their digital literacy and resilience (Livingstone et al., 2017).

Furthermore, parental guidance involves fostering open communication and trust between parents and children, creating a supportive and responsive environment where children feel comfortable sharing their concerns, experiences, and questions about digital technology (Livingstone et al., 2017). By maintaining open lines of communication and listening attentively to children's perspectives and needs, parents can build strong relationships based on mutual respect, empathy, and understanding, enabling them to address challenges and resolve conflicts related to digital technology collaboratively (Livingstone et al., 2017). Additionally, parents can use technology as a tool for communication and connection, staying connected with their children through messaging apps, video calls, and social media platforms, even when they are apart (Livingstone et al., 2017).

In conclusion, parental guidance in a digital age is essential for supporting children's healthy development and well-being in an increasingly connected and technology-driven world. By setting clear boundaries, monitoring online activities, modeling positive behaviors, promoting digital literacy, fostering open communication, and building trusting relationships, parents can empower children to navigate the digital landscape safely, responsibly, and ethically (Livingstone et al., 2017).

Strategies for Navigating AI's Influence on Parenting

Navigating AI's influence on parenting requires thoughtful consideration and proactive strategies to harness the benefits while mitigating potential risks. One key strategy is to stay informed and educated about AI technologies and their implications for parenting practices (Livingstone et al., 2017). By staying abreast of developments in AI-driven parenting tools, such as monitoring apps, virtual assistants, and AI-driven toys, parents can make informed decisions about their use and evaluate their potential impact on children's well-being and development.

Moreover, parents can establish clear boundaries and guidelines for the use of AI-driven technologies in parenting, setting limits on screen time, data sharing, and online interactions (Livingstone et al., 2017). By defining clear expectations and rules around the use of AI-driven tools, parents can ensure that children's privacy, safety, and autonomy are respected and protected (Livingstone et al., 2017). Additionally, parents can model responsible and mindful technology use, demonstrating healthy screen habits and digital etiquette in their own interactions with AI-driven devices and platforms (Livingstone et al., 2017).

Furthermore, parents can actively engage with AI-driven parenting tools and platforms, leveraging their capabilities to support and enhance their parenting practices (Livingstone et al., 2017). For example, AI-powered monitoring apps can provide insights into children's digital activities and behaviors, allowing parents to identify potential risks, set appropriate limits, and initiate conversations about online safety and responsible digital citizenship (Livingstone et al., 2017). Additionally, AI-driven educational apps and games can offer personalized learning experiences tailored to children's individual interests, abilities, and learning styles, supplementing traditional educational approaches and fostering children's academic success (Livingstone et al., 2017).

Moreover, parents can foster critical thinking and digital literacy skills in their children, empowering them to navigate and evaluate AI-driven content and information effectively (Livingstone et al., 2017). By teaching children how to assess the credibility, reliability, and bias of AI-generated content, parents can help them develop media literacy and discernment, enabling them to make informed decisions and avoid misinformation, fake news, and online scams (Livingstone et al., 2017). Additionally, parents can encourage children to question, analyze, and reflect critically on the ethical implications of AI technologies, promoting a deeper understanding of their societal impact and ethical considerations (Livingstone et al., 2017).

Furthermore, parents can foster open communication and trust with their children, creating a supportive and responsive environment where children feel comfortable sharing their thoughts, concerns, and questions about AI-driven technologies (Livingstone et al., 2017). By maintaining open lines of communication and listening attentively to children's perspectives and experiences, parents can build strong relationships based on mutual respect, empathy, and understanding, enabling them to address challenges and concerns related to AI's influence on parenting collaboratively (Livingstone et al., 2017).

In conclusion, navigating AI's influence on parenting requires proactive strategies that prioritize children's well-being, privacy, and development. By staying informed, setting clear boundaries, engaging with AI-driven tools thoughtfully, fostering critical thinking and digital literacy skills, and maintaining open communication and trust with children, parents can navigate the complexities of parenting in the digital age and harness the transformative potential of AI technologies for their children's growth and success (Livingstone et al., 2017).

Balancing Tech Use and Real-Life Experiences

Balancing technology use with real-life experiences is essential for maintaining a healthy and well-rounded lifestyle, particularly in today's digital age. While technology offers numerous benefits and conveniences, excessive screen time and reliance on digital devices can detract from real-world interactions, physical activity, and meaningful experiences. One key strategy for achieving balance is to establish clear boundaries and limits around technology use, ensuring that it complements rather than dominates daily routines (Radesky et al., 2015). By setting guidelines for screen time, device-free zones, and offline activities, individuals and families can create space for real-life experiences that promote social connections, physical health, and emotional well-being.

Moreover, fostering mindfulness and intentionality in technology use can help individuals and families prioritize meaningful interactions and experiences over mindless scrolling and digital distractions (Radesky et al., 2015). By cultivating awareness of how and why technology is being used, individuals can make conscious choices about when to engage with digital devices and when to disconnect in favor of real-life interactions and activities. Additionally, practicing digital detoxes and periodic breaks from screens can help reset habits and restore balance, allowing individuals to reconnect with themselves and their surroundings (Radesky et al., 2015).

Furthermore, promoting a healthy balance between technology use and real-life experiences requires diversifying leisure activities and interests to encompass both digital and non-digital pursuits (Uhls et al., 2014). Encouraging hobbies such as outdoor play, sports, arts and crafts, and reading can provide opportunities for hands-on learning, creativity, and socialization that complement screen-based activities (Uhls et al., 2014). By offering a variety of experiences and outlets for self-expression, individuals can find fulfillment and satisfaction in both digital and real-world contexts, fostering a well-rounded lifestyle.

Additionally, fostering strong interpersonal connections and relationships offline is essential for maintaining balance and well-being in the digital age (Uhls et al., 2014). Spending quality time with family and friends, engaging in face-to-face conversations, and participating in shared activities and experiences can strengthen bonds and provide a sense of belonging and connection that transcends digital interactions (Uhls et al., 2014). Prioritizing social interactions and meaningful connections can help individuals maintain perspective and balance in their lives, even as technology continues to play a significant role in daily routines.

Moreover, integrating technology into real-life experiences in purposeful and meaningful ways can enhance learning, creativity, and productivity (Uhls et al., 2014). For example, using digital tools and resources to support hobbies, interests, and passions can enrich experiences and expand possibilities for exploration and discovery. Whether it's using digital photography to document outdoor adventures, leveraging online platforms to connect with like-minded individuals, or utilizing productivity apps to manage tasks and goals, technology can complement and enhance real-life experiences when used intentionally and mindfully (Uhls et al., 2014).

Furthermore, promoting digital literacy and responsible technology use is essential for empowering individuals to navigate the complexities of the digital world and make informed choices about their technology use (Radesky et al., 2015). Educating children and adults about the potential risks and benefits of technology, teaching critical thinking skills for evaluating online information, and fostering digital citizenship and ethical behavior can help individuals develop the skills and competencies needed to use technology responsibly and effectively (Radesky et al., 2015).

In conclusion, balancing technology use with real-life experiences requires intentionality, mindfulness, and a thoughtful approach to incorporating technology into daily routines. By setting boundaries, fostering mindfulness, diversifying leisure activities, prioritizing interpersonal connections, integrating technology purposefully, and promoting digital literacy, individuals and families can strike a healthy balance between digital and non-digital pursuits, leading to a more fulfilling and well-rounded lifestyle (Radesky et al., 2015; Uhls et al., 2014).

Chapter 8

Educators and AI: Transforming Early Learning Environments

Integrating AI into Early Childhood Education

Integrating Artificial Intelligence (AI) into early childhood education holds promise for enhancing learning experiences and outcomes for young children. One approach is the development of AI-powered educational platforms that offer personalized learning experiences tailored to individual children's needs, preferences, and learning styles (VanLehn, 2011). By analyzing data on children's interactions and performance, AI algorithms can adapt content, pacing, and feedback to optimize learning experiences and promote skill development (VanLehn, 2011). This personalized approach to learning can foster engagement, motivation, and academic success in young learners.

Furthermore, AI technologies can support educators in delivering differentiated instruction and interventions that address the diverse needs and abilities of children in early childhood classrooms (VanLehn, 2011). For example, AI-driven tutoring systems can provide adaptive support and scaffolding to help struggling learners master concepts and skills at their own pace (VanLehn, 2011). Similarly, AI-powered assessment tools can generate real-time insights into children's progress and areas for growth, enabling educators to tailor instructional strategies and interventions accordingly (VanLehn, 2011). By leveraging AI technologies, educators can provide targeted support that meets the unique learning needs of each child.

Moreover, AI-driven educational games and simulations offer immersive and interactive learning experiences that engage children's curiosity, creativity, and problem-solving skills (Holmes et al., 2019). By integrating AI algorithms into game design, developers can create dynamic and adaptive gameplay experiences that challenge children to think critically, explore new concepts, and apply their knowledge in contextually relevant ways (Holmes et al., 2019). Additionally, AI-powered virtual tutors and characters can provide personalized feedback, guidance, and encouragement as children navigate learning challenges and activities within the game environment (Holmes et al., 2019).

Additionally, AI technologies can facilitate early identification and intervention for children at risk for developmental delays or learning difficulties (VanLehn, 2011). By analyzing patterns and trends in children's interactions and behaviors, AI algorithms can flag potential concerns and alert educators and caregivers to areas that may require further assessment or support (VanLehn, 2011). Early intervention is critical for addressing developmental delays and mitigating long-term academic and social-emotional challenges, and AI-powered tools can play a valuable role in this process.

Furthermore, AI-driven natural language processing (NLP) technologies enable interactive dialogue and communication between young children and virtual tutors or chatbots (Holmes et al., 2019). Through conversational interactions, children engage in language-rich environments that promote linguistic development, vocabulary acquisition, and comprehension skills (Holmes et al.,

2019). AI-driven language learning applications offer opportunities for children to practice speaking, listening, and communicating in a supportive and interactive setting, enhancing their language fluency and proficiency (Holmes et al., 2019).

Moreover, AI technologies can support early literacy development by providing adaptive and personalized literacy instruction and support (Holmes et al., 2019). For example, AI-powered reading programs can analyze children's reading abilities and preferences, offering leveled texts, comprehension activities, and vocabulary exercises tailored to their individual needs (Holmes et al., 2019). Additionally, AI-driven language learning apps can incorporate game-based elements, interactive storytelling, and multimedia resources to engage children in literacy-rich experiences that promote a love of reading and learning (Holmes et al., 2019).

Additionally, AI technologies can facilitate collaboration and communication among educators, parents, and caregivers, fostering a holistic and integrated approach to early childhood education (Holmes et al., 2019). AI-powered platforms and tools can streamline administrative tasks, generate insights into children's progress and development, and facilitate communication and collaboration among stakeholders (Holmes et al., 2019). By connecting educators, parents, and caregivers in a shared learning community, AI technologies can support continuity and coherence in children's learning experiences across home and school settings (Holmes et al., 2019).

In conclusion, integrating AI into early childhood education has the potential to transform learning experiences and outcomes for young children. By providing personalized learning experiences, supporting differentiated instruction and interventions, facilitating early identification and intervention for developmental delays, promoting language and literacy development, and fostering collaboration and communication among stakeholders, AI technologies can empower educators, parents, and caregivers to create enriching and supportive learning environments that meet the diverse needs of young learners.

Professional Development for Educators in AI Integration

Professional development for educators in AI integration is crucial for preparing teachers to effectively leverage AI technologies in educational settings. One approach to professional development is providing educators with hands-on training and workshops that familiarize them with AI tools and platforms relevant to their subject areas and teaching contexts (Wang et al., 2020). Through interactive and experiential learning experiences, educators can gain practical skills and knowledge in using AI-driven educational resources, such as adaptive learning systems, virtual tutors, and data analytics tools, to enhance teaching and learning (Wang et al., 2020).

Furthermore, professional development programs can offer opportunities for educators to explore pedagogical strategies and instructional practices that leverage AI technologies to meet the diverse needs of learners (Wang et al., 2020). For example, workshops on differentiated instruction, personalized learning, and data-driven decision-making can help educators design and implement AI-supported teaching approaches that address individual students' strengths, interests, and learning styles (Wang et al., 2020). By providing guidance on how to integrate AI tools into lesson planning, assessment, and feedback practices, professional development programs can empower educators to create inclusive and engaging learning environments.

Moreover, professional development initiatives can promote collaboration and knowledge sharing among educators, enabling them to learn from each other's experiences and expertise in AI integration (Wang et al., 2020). Collaborative learning communities, online forums, and peer mentoring programs can facilitate dialogue, reflection, and collaboration among educators as they explore innovative ways to incorporate AI technologies into their teaching practices (Wang et al., 2020). By fostering a culture of collaboration and continuous learning, professional development initiatives can support educators in staying abreast of emerging trends and best practices in AI integration.

Additionally, professional development programs can address educators' concerns and misconceptions about AI technologies, providing information and resources to help them navigate ethical, privacy, and equity issues related to AI integration in education (Wang et al., 2020). Workshops on data privacy, algorithmic bias, and digital citizenship can equip educators with the knowledge and skills needed to promote responsible and ethical use of AI tools and platforms in educational settings (Wang et al., 2020). By addressing educators' concerns and providing guidance on ethical considerations, professional development programs can build confidence and competence in AI integration.

Furthermore, professional development initiatives can offer ongoing support and mentorship to educators as they navigate the complexities of AI integration in their teaching practices (Wang et al., 2020). Follow-up workshops, coaching sessions, and online resources can provide educators with continued guidance and assistance as they experiment with AI technologies, reflect on their experiences, and refine their instructional approaches (Wang et al., 2020). Additionally, access to technical support and troubleshooting resources can help educators overcome challenges and barriers to AI integration, ensuring a smooth and successful implementation process.

Moreover, professional development programs can foster a culture of innovation and experimentation in education, encouraging educators to explore new technologies and teaching methods that enhance student engagement and learning outcomes (Wang et al., 2020). By providing opportunities for educators to experiment with AI tools and platforms in a supportive and risk-free environment, professional development initiatives can spark creativity, curiosity, and enthusiasm for innovation (Wang et al., 2020). Additionally, recognition and celebration of educators' achievements and successes in AI integration can inspire others to embrace new possibilities and pursue excellence in teaching and learning.

In conclusion, professional development for educators in AI integration plays a vital role in preparing teachers to effectively leverage AI technologies to enhance teaching and learning. By providing hands-on training, promoting pedagogical innovation, fostering collaboration and knowledge sharing, addressing ethical concerns, offering ongoing support and mentorship, and fostering a culture of experimentation and innovation, professional development programs can empower educators to harness the transformative potential of AI in education.

Ethical Considerations and Best Practices

Ethical considerations and best practices are paramount in various fields, from healthcare to technology, education, and beyond. In the realm of artificial intelligence (AI), these considerations become even more critical due to the potential impact of AI systems on individuals, societies, and the environment. One ethical consideration is the principle of fairness and equity in AI algorithms and decision-making processes (Mittelstadt et al., 2016). AI systems must be designed and trained to avoid bias and discrimination based on factors such as race, gender, ethnicity, or socioeconomic status. By ensuring fairness in AI systems, we can promote equality and justice in decision-making processes across diverse populations.

Transparency and accountability are also essential ethical principles in AI development and deployment (Floridi et al., 2018). AI systems should be transparent about their decision-making processes, data sources, and potential limitations, enabling users to understand how decisions are made and to hold developers and operators accountable for their actions. By promoting transparency and accountability, we can foster trust and confidence in AI technologies and mitigate concerns about opacity and algorithmic bias.

Privacy and data protection are fundamental ethical considerations in AI, given the vast amounts of personal data collected, processed, and analyzed by AI systems (Jobin et al., 2019). AI developers and operators must prioritize data privacy and security, implementing robust measures to protect sensitive information and ensure compliance with data protection regulations such as the General Data Protection Regulation (GDPR) and the Health Insurance Portability and Accountability Act (HIPAA). By safeguarding privacy and data security, we can uphold individuals' rights to autonomy, confidentiality, and consent in the digital age.

Another ethical consideration in AI is the potential for unintended consequences and unforeseen risks associated with AI technologies (Bostrom & Yudkowsky, 2014). AI systems may exhibit unexpected behaviors or outcomes that can have far-reaching implications for individuals and society. Therefore, developers and operators must anticipate and mitigate potential risks through rigorous testing, validation, and risk assessment processes. By proactively addressing risks and uncertainties, we can minimize harm and maximize the beneficial impact of AI technologies.

Moreover, ethical AI development requires interdisciplinary collaboration and engagement with diverse stakeholders, including ethicists, policymakers, technologists, and affected communities (Floridi et al., 2018). By fostering dialogue and collaboration among stakeholders, we can ensure that ethical considerations are integrated into all stages of the AI lifecycle, from design and development to deployment and evaluation. This participatory approach can help identify and address ethical concerns early in the development process and promote responsible and inclusive AI innovation.

In addition to ethical principles, best practices in AI development and deployment are essential for promoting the responsible and effective use of AI technologies (Floridi et al., 2018). One best practice is to prioritize human-centered design and user engagement, ensuring that AI systems are designed to meet users' needs, preferences, and capabilities (Jobin et al., 2019). By involving end-users in the design and development process, developers can create AI systems that are intuitive, user-friendly, and aligned with user expectations and values.

Furthermore, ongoing monitoring and evaluation are critical best practices in AI deployment, enabling developers and operators to assess the performance, impact, and ethical implications of AI systems over time (Floridi et al., 2018). Continuous monitoring and evaluation allow for the detection of potential biases, errors, or adverse effects of AI systems, prompting corrective actions and improvements as needed. By implementing robust monitoring and evaluation mechanisms, we can ensure that AI technologies remain ethical, accountable, and aligned with societal values and goals.

Additionally, fostering a culture of responsible innovation and ethical leadership is essential for promoting ethical AI practices within organizations and across industries (Floridi et al., 2018). Leaders and decision-makers must prioritize ethical considerations in AI development and deployment, setting clear ethical guidelines, standards, and policies that govern the responsible use of AI technologies (Jobin et al., 2019). By promoting ethical leadership and organizational culture, we can create environments where ethical AI practices are valued, supported, and upheld by all stakeholders.

In conclusion, ethical considerations and best practices are essential for guiding the development, deployment, and use of AI technologies in a responsible and ethical manner. By prioritizing fairness, transparency, privacy, risk mitigation, interdisciplinary collaboration, human-centered design, monitoring and evaluation, and ethical leadership, we can ensure that AI technologies contribute positively to society while minimizing potential harms and risks

Chapter 9
Beyond the Classroom: AI and Early Childhood Policy

Policy Implications of AI in Early Childhood

The integration of Artificial Intelligence (AI) in early childhood education raises significant policy implications that need careful consideration to ensure ethical, equitable, and effective implementation. One key policy consideration is the need for comprehensive guidelines and regulations governing the development, deployment, and use of AI technologies in early childhood settings (McCoy et al., 2021). Policymakers must establish clear standards and criteria for evaluating AI systems' safety, efficacy, and appropriateness for use with young children, taking into account factors such as data privacy, algorithmic bias, and developmental appropriateness.

Moreover, policymakers should prioritize investments in research and development to advance AI technologies specifically tailored to the needs and developmental stages of young children (McCoy et al., 2021). Funding initiatives and grants can support interdisciplinary collaborations between researchers, educators, technologists, and child development experts to develop AI-driven educational tools and platforms that promote positive learning outcomes for young children. By investing in research and development, policymakers can ensure that AI technologies in early childhood education are evidence-based, culturally responsive, and aligned with best practices in child development.

Additionally, policymakers must address digital equity and access issues to ensure that all children, regardless of socioeconomic status or geographical location, have equitable access to AI-driven educational resources and opportunities (McCoy et al., 2021). This may involve initiatives to bridge the digital divide by expanding broadband infrastructure, providing subsidized technology devices and internet access to underserved communities, and promoting digital literacy and skills development among children and families. By prioritizing digital equity, policymakers can help mitigate disparities in access to high-quality early childhood education and support the educational needs of all children.

Furthermore, policymakers should consider the ethical implications of AI technologies in early childhood education and develop policies and guidelines to safeguard children's privacy, safety, and well-being (McCoy et al., 2021). This may include regulations to protect children's personal data from unauthorized access or misuse, guidelines for obtaining parental consent for data collection and usage, and protocols for addressing algorithmic bias and discrimination in AI systems. By enacting robust privacy and ethical standards, policymakers can ensure that AI technologies in early childhood education adhere to ethical principles and respect children's rights and dignity.

In addition to regulatory measures, policymakers should promote professional development and capacity-building initiatives to empower educators and caregivers to effectively integrate AI technologies into early childhood education (McCoy et al., 2021). This may involve funding training programs, workshops, and professional learning communities that provide educators with the knowledge, skills, and resources needed to use AI-driven educational tools and platforms responsibly and ethically. By investing in professional development, policymakers can support educators in leveraging AI technologies to enhance teaching practices, personalize learning experiences, and meet the diverse needs of young children.

Moreover, policymakers should foster collaboration and knowledge-sharing among stakeholders in the early childhood education ecosystem, including educators, researchers, policymakers, parents, and technology developers (McCoy et al., 2021). Collaborative initiatives and partnerships can facilitate the exchange of best practices, research findings, and lessons learned in AI integration, enabling stakeholders to learn from each other's experiences and work together to address common challenges and opportunities. By fostering collaboration, policymakers can promote innovation, continuous improvement, and collective impact in early childhood education.

Furthermore, policymakers should promote research and evaluation efforts to assess the impact and effectiveness of AI technologies in early childhood education (McCoy et al., 2021). Longitudinal studies randomized controlled trials, and qualitative research can provide valuable insights into the benefits, challenges, and unintended consequences of AI integration, informing evidence-based policymaking and practice. By investing in research and evaluation, policymakers can ensure that AI technologies in early childhood education are informed by empirical evidence and contribute to positive outcomes for children.

Additionally, policymakers should engage with stakeholders in ongoing dialogue and consultation processes to solicit feedback, address concerns, and adapt policies and regulations as needed to reflect evolving developments and emerging issues in AI integration (McCoy et al., 2021). Open and transparent communication channels can foster trust, collaboration, and accountability among stakeholders, enabling policymakers to make informed decisions that align with the needs and priorities of the early childhood education community. By engaging stakeholders in policymaking processes, policymakers can promote inclusivity, responsiveness, and democratic governance in AI integration.

In conclusion, the policy implications of AI in early childhood education are multifaceted and complex, requiring thoughtful consideration and proactive action from policymakers to ensure responsible and equitable implementation. By prioritizing regulatory oversight, research and development, digital equity, ethical considerations, professional development, collaboration, research and evaluation, and stakeholder engagement, policymakers can create an enabling environment for harnessing the potential of AI technologies to enhance early childhood education and support the holistic development of young children.

Ensuring Equity and Access in AI-Driven Early Childhood Initiatives

Ensuring equity and access in AI-driven early childhood initiatives is paramount for promoting inclusive education and fostering positive outcomes for all children, regardless of their background or circumstances. One key consideration is addressing disparities in access to technology and digital resources among underserved communities (Warschauer, 2019). Policymakers and education stakeholders must prioritize efforts to bridge the digital divide by providing equitable access to technology devices, internet connectivity, and AI-driven educational tools and platforms in low-income neighborhoods, rural areas, and marginalized communities.

Furthermore, efforts to promote equity in AI-driven early childhood initiatives must address cultural and linguistic diversity to ensure that educational content and resources are inclusive and relevant to the diverse backgrounds and experiences of children and families (Lee & Searson, 2020). This may involve developing culturally responsive AI algorithms, multilingual interfaces, and culturally relevant content that reflect the linguistic, cultural, and socio-economic diversity of the communities served. By embracing cultural diversity, AI-driven early childhood initiatives can empower children to see themselves reflected in their learning experiences and promote a sense of belonging and identity affirmation.

Additionally, policymakers and education leaders must prioritize efforts to mitigate biases and discrimination in AI algorithms and decision-making processes to ensure equitable outcomes for all children (Crawford et al., 2019). AI systems are susceptible to algorithmic bias, which can perpetuate existing inequalities and exacerbate disparities in educational opportunities. Therefore, it is essential to implement robust measures for detecting, mitigating, and preventing bias in AI-driven early childhood initiatives, such as algorithmic audits, bias impact assessments, and diversity-aware training data collection practices.

Moreover, promoting equity in AI-driven early childhood initiatives requires a holistic approach that addresses not only access to technology but also broader social determinants of educational equity, such as poverty, housing instability, and systemic discrimination (Hughes-Hassell &Mancall, 2021). Efforts to promote equity must include strategies for addressing the underlying structural inequities that perpetuate disparities in educational opportunities and outcomes, such as targeted investments in early childhood education, healthcare, housing, and community development initiatives that support children and families in marginalized communities.

Furthermore, fostering partnerships and collaboration among stakeholders in the public, private, and nonprofit sectors is essential for advancing equity and access in AI-driven early childhood initiatives (Lee & Searson, 2020). Collaborative efforts can leverage the expertise, resources, and networks of diverse stakeholders to develop and implement innovative solutions that address the complex and interconnected challenges of educational equity. By working together, stakeholders can amplify their impact, share best practices, and coordinate efforts to ensure that AI-driven early childhood initiatives reach and benefit all children.

Additionally, community engagement and participatory approaches are essential for promoting equity and ensuring that AI-driven early childhood initiatives are responsive to the needs and priorities of the communities they serve (Hughes-Hassell &Mancall, 2021). Engaging parents, caregivers, community leaders, and other stakeholders in decision-making processes can help ensure that initiatives are culturally relevant, linguistically appropriate, and responsive to the unique strengths and assets of the community. By centering the voices and experiences of the community, AI-driven early childhood initiatives can build trust, foster collaboration, and promote sustainable solutions that address local needs and priorities.

Moreover, ongoing monitoring, evaluation, and accountability mechanisms are essential for assessing the impact and effectiveness of AI-driven early childhood initiatives in promoting equity and access (Crawford et al., 2019). Regular evaluations can help identify disparities, gaps, and areas for improvement in program implementation and outcomes, enabling stakeholders to make data-driven decisions and course corrections as needed. Additionally, transparency and accountability mechanisms can promote trust and confidence among stakeholders by providing visibility into decision-making processes, resource allocation, and program outcomes.

In conclusion, ensuring equity and access in AI-driven early childhood initiatives requires a multifaceted and collaborative approach that addresses systemic barriers, promotes cultural responsiveness, mitigates bias, fosters community engagement, and prioritizes ongoing monitoring and evaluation. By prioritizing equity and access in the design, implementation, and evaluation of AI-driven early childhood initiatives, policymakers, educators, and stakeholders can work together to create inclusive learning environments that empower all children to thrive and reach their full potential.

Advocacy and Future Directions

Advocacy plays a crucial role in shaping the future directions of AI-driven initiatives in various fields, including education, healthcare, and governance. Advocates advocate for policies, practices, and resources that promote equity, access, and ethical use of AI technologies (Lomas, 2021). They work to raise awareness about the potential benefits and risks of AI, engage stakeholders in meaningful dialogue, and mobilize support for initiatives that prioritize the well-being and rights of individuals and communities.

Moreover, advocacy efforts seek to empower marginalized and underrepresented groups to participate in decision-making processes and shape the development and deployment of AI technologies (Haque, 2020). By amplifying the voices and experiences of those most affected by AI-driven initiatives, advocates can ensure that policies and practices are informed by diverse perspectives and responsive to the needs and priorities of all stakeholders.

Furthermore, advocacy plays a critical role in holding policymakers, industry stakeholders, and other actors accountable for their actions and commitments related to AI ethics, transparency, and accountability (Mittelstadt et al., 2016). Advocates monitor developments in AI governance, track compliance with regulations and standards, and advocate for greater transparency, oversight, and enforcement mechanisms to prevent abuses of power and protect individuals' rights.

In addition to advocacy at the policy level, grassroots advocacy efforts mobilize communities and individuals to take action on issues related to AI ethics, bias, and social justice (Benjamin, 2019). Grassroots organizations, activist groups, and community organizers work to educate the public, raise awareness about AI-related issues, and mobilize support for initiatives that promote equity, fairness, and human rights in the use of AI technologies.

Furthermore, advocacy efforts focus on fostering interdisciplinary collaboration and knowledge-sharing among stakeholders from diverse backgrounds and fields (Floridi et al., 2018). By bringing together experts in AI ethics, law, policy, sociology, and other disciplines, advocates can generate new insights, perspectives, and solutions to complex ethical and social challenges posed by AI technologies.

Moreover, advocacy plays a vital role in shaping public discourse and narratives around AI, challenging misconceptions, and promoting informed dialogue (Crawford, 2020). Advocates engage with the media, policymakers, and the public to debunk myths and stereotypes about AI, highlight ethical concerns and human rights implications, and advocate for a more nuanced and critical understanding of AI technologies and their impact on society.

Additionally, advocacy efforts promote education and capacity-building initiatives to empower individuals and communities to navigate the ethical, social, and policy implications of AI (Jobin et al., 2019). Advocates develop resources, training programs, and educational materials to increase awareness and understanding of AI ethics, data privacy, algorithmic bias, and other relevant topics, equipping people with the knowledge and skills needed to advocate for ethical and responsible AI use.

Furthermore, advocacy efforts focus on fostering international collaboration and cooperation to address global challenges and opportunities posed by AI technologies (Lomas, 2021). Advocates advocate for the development of international norms, standards, and guidelines for AI governance, data sharing, and technology transfer, promoting a shared understanding of ethical principles and best practices across borders.

Moreover, advocacy plays a crucial role in promoting diversity, equity, and inclusion in the AI workforce and research community (Lee & Searson, 2020). Advocates work to address systemic barriers and biases that limit opportunities for underrepresented groups in AI education, employment, and leadership roles, advocating for policies and practices that promote diversity and inclusivity in AI research, development, and deployment.

In conclusion, advocacy is essential for shaping the future directions of AI-driven initiatives and ensuring that AI technologies are developed, deployed, and governed in ways that promote equity, fairness, and human rights. By advocating for policies, practices, and resources that prioritize ethical use, transparency, and accountability in AI, advocates can help build a more inclusive and sustainable future for all.

Chapter 10

Conclusion: Shaping a Bright Future for Early Childhood in the Age of AI

Reflections on the Intersection of AI and Early Childhood

Excitement and caution mingle at the intersection of AI and early childhood as we navigate the potentials and pitfalls of integrating advanced technologies into the formative years of a child's development. At its core, AI offers opportunities to revolutionize early childhood education, providing personalized learning experiences that cater to individual needs, interests, and learning styles (Wang et al., 2020). However, as we delve deeper into this intersection, it becomes imperative to tread carefully, considering ethical, developmental, and societal implications.

Ethical considerations inherent in utilizing AI technologies with young children evoke thoughtful deliberation. AI-driven systems have the potential to collect vast amounts of data on children's behaviors, preferences, and interactions, raising concerns about privacy, consent, and data protection (Floridi et al., 2018). Ensuring that AI applications in early childhood are designed and implemented in a manner that respects children's rights, autonomy, and well-being is paramount.

Understanding the developmental needs and capabilities of young learners is essential in reflections on the intersection of AI and early childhood. While AI has the capacity to deliver tailored learning experiences, it is crucial to ensure that these experiences align with children's developmental stages and foster holistic growth (Lee & Searson, 2020). Designing and implementing AI-driven educational interventions that are developmentally appropriate and supportive of children's cognitive, social, emotional, and physical development is paramount.

Human-technology interaction takes center stage in reflections on the intersection of AI and early childhood. Rather than replacing human interaction and guidance, AI should complement and enhance the role of educators, caregivers, and peers in children's learning and development (Lillard et al., 2015). Prioritizing the human aspect of education while harnessing the potential of technology to augment and amplify learning opportunities is crucial.

Broader societal implications of AI-driven education warrant reflection at the intersection of AI and early childhood. As AI technologies become increasingly integrated into educational settings, it is essential to address issues of digital equity, access, and inclusion (Hughes-Hassell &Mancall, 2021). Advocating for policies and initiatives that promote equitable access to technology and support the diverse needs of children and families is imperative.

The role of algorithms and data in shaping children's learning experiences and outcomes prompts critical examination in reflections on the intersection of AI and early childhood. AI-driven systems rely on algorithms to analyze data and make decisions about content delivery, assessment, and feedback (Warschauer, 2019). Mitigating bias, promoting diversity, and fostering inclusive learning environments in AI technologies are crucial considerations.

Adapting educators' roles and responsibilities to effectively integrate AI into their practice is another aspect to reflect upon at the intersection of AI and early childhood (Lee & Searson, 2020). Investing in professional development, training, and support mechanisms to empower educators to harness the potential of AI technologies while maintaining their pedagogical autonomy and expertise is essential.

Ongoing research and evaluation to understand the impact of AI-driven education on children's learning outcomes, socio-emotional development, and well-being demand reflection (Crawford, 2020). Reflecting on research findings and evidence-based practices can inform the design and implementation of AI-driven interventions that maximize benefits and minimize risks for young learners.

In conclusion, navigating the complex terrain at the intersection of AI and early childhood requires mindfulness, critical inquiry, and a commitment to ethical, inclusive, and holistic approaches to education. Engaging in reflective practice allows us to harness the transformative potential of AI technologies while safeguarding children's rights, promoting equitable access, and nurturing their holistic development.

Key Takeaways and Recommendations

In the journey of exploring the intersection of AI and early childhood, one of the primary considerations lies in upholding ethical principles. As we embark on this path, it's essential to prioritize privacy, consent, and data protection to ensure the well-being and rights of children are safeguarded. Furthermore, aligning AI-driven learning experiences with children's developmental stages emerges as a crucial aspect. By tailoring interventions that support cognitive, social, emotional, and physical development, we can create educational environments that are nurturing and conducive to growth.

In our narrative, the role of human-technology interaction takes center stage. While AI offers innovative opportunities for learning, educators and caregivers remain indispensable in providing guidance, support, and meaningful interactions. They play a pivotal role in nurturing children's agency, creativity, and socio-emotional development, ensuring that technology complements rather than replaces human connection.

As we navigate this terrain, addressing issues of digital equity and access becomes paramount. Advocating for policies and initiatives that promote equitable access to technology ensures that all children have the opportunity to benefit from AI-driven learning experiences. Moreover, mitigating biases in AI algorithms and data is crucial for fostering fairness, diversity, and inclusivity in educational settings. By implementing measures to detect and prevent bias, we can create learning environments that promote equal opportunities for all children.

Empowering educators emerges as a key theme in our narrative. Investing in professional development, training, and support mechanisms enables educators to leverage AI technologies effectively while maintaining their pedagogical autonomy and expertise. Additionally, supporting ongoing research and evaluation efforts helps us understand the impact of AI-driven education on children's learning outcomes and well-being. By fostering collaboration between researchers, educators, and policymakers, we can generate evidence-based insights that inform the design and implementation of AI-driven interventions.

Community engagement and global collaboration are essential elements in our narrative. Involving stakeholders in decision-making processes and co-designing interventions ensures that AI-driven initiatives are responsive to the diverse needs and priorities of children, families, and communities. By sharing best practices, research findings, and resources across borders, we can advance equity, accessibility, and quality in early childhood education on a global scale.

Finally, our narrative emphasizes the importance of continuous reflection and improvement. Regularly assessing the impact, effectiveness, and ethical implications of AI technologies allows us to adapt practices and policies in response to emerging challenges and opportunities. By fostering a culture of reflection and learning, we can navigate the intersection of AI and early childhood with mindfulness, critical inquiry, and a commitment to ethical, inclusive, and holistic approaches to education.

Looking Ahead: Opportunities and Challenges Looking ahead, the intersection of AI and various domains presents both promising opportunities and complex challenges that warrant careful consideration and proactive strategies for mitigation. As AI continues to evolve and permeate various aspects of society, including education, healthcare, and governance, it offers the potential to revolutionize how we address critical issues and enhance human capabilities (Russell & Norvig, 2021).

In education, AI holds the promise of personalized learning experiences tailored to individual student needs and preferences. Adaptive learning platforms powered by AI algorithms can analyze vast amounts of data to provide targeted support and feedback, optimizing learning outcomes (Koedinger et al., 2012). By harnessing AI technologies, educators can create more engaging and effective learning environments that cater to diverse learning styles and abilities.

Moreover, AI-driven advancements in healthcare present opportunities for more accurate diagnostics, personalized treatment plans, and improved patient outcomes. Machine learning algorithms can analyze medical imaging data, genetic information, and clinical records to identify patterns and trends that may go unnoticed by human clinicians (Esteva et al., 2019). By leveraging AI, healthcare providers can make more informed decisions, leading to earlier interventions and better health outcomes for patients.

In the realm of governance and public administration, AI offers the potential to enhance efficiency, transparency, and decision-making processes. Predictive analytics and data-driven insights can inform policy development, resource allocation, and service delivery, enabling governments to address complex challenges more effectively (Lazer et al., 2020). By embracing AI technologies, policymakers can improve the quality of public services, promote civic engagement, and foster more inclusive and responsive governance structures.

However, alongside these opportunities, the widespread adoption of AI also raises significant challenges and concerns that must be addressed. One major concern is the potential for AI algorithms to perpetuate or exacerbate biases and inequalities present in the data they are trained on (Crawford, 2016). Biases in AI systems can lead to unfair outcomes, discrimination, and exacerbation of social disparities, particularly in sensitive domains such as criminal justice, hiring, and lending.

Furthermore, the increasing reliance on AI technologies raises questions about accountability, transparency, and ethical use. As AI systems become more complex and autonomous, it becomes challenging to understand and explain their decision-making processes (Rudin, 2019). This lack of transparency can undermine trust in AI technologies and raise concerns about their fairness, reliability, and potential unintended consequences.

Moreover, the rapid pace of technological advancement in AI poses challenges for policymakers, regulators, and society at large in keeping pace with developments and ensuring responsible and ethical use of AI technologies (Brynjolfsson & McAfee, 2017). Regulatory frameworks and governance mechanisms must evolve to address emerging risks and ethical dilemmas associated with AI, such as data privacy, algorithmic accountability, and the impact on employment and labor markets.

Another significant challenge is the potential for AI technologies to disrupt existing industries and labor markets, leading to job displacement and economic dislocation for workers in certain sectors (Autor et al., 2020). As AI automation accelerates, policymakers and stakeholders must consider strategies for upskilling and reskilling the workforce, promoting job creation in emerging sectors, and ensuring a just transition to the digital economy.

Furthermore, the ethical implications of AI extend beyond technical considerations to encompass broader societal values and norms. Questions about the ethical use of AI, including issues related to fairness, accountability, transparency, and privacy, require interdisciplinary collaboration and public engagement to develop consensus and establish norms and standards for responsible AI development and deployment (Floridi et al., 2018).

In addressing these challenges and opportunities, interdisciplinary collaboration and stakeholder engagement are essential. By bringing together experts from diverse fields, including computer science, ethics, social sciences, and policy, we can develop holistic and contextually relevant approaches to AI governance and regulation (Jobin et al., 2019). Moreover, engaging with a broad range of stakeholders, including policymakers, industry leaders, civil society organizations, and the general public, can foster greater awareness, understanding, and consensus around AI issues and promote responsible and ethical AI innovation (Brundage et al., 2020).

In conclusion, the intersection of AI presents both promising opportunities and complex challenges that require careful consideration and proactive strategies for mitigation. By harnessing the potential of AI technologies while addressing ethical, social, and economic concerns, we can unlock the transformative potential of AI to benefit individuals, communities, and society as a whole.

References

Autor, D. H., Mindell, D., & Reynolds, E. (2020). The Work of the Future: Building Better Jobs in an Age of Intelligent Machines. Princeton University Press.

Brundage, M., Avin, S., Clark, J., Toner, H., Eckersley, P., Garfinkel, B., ... & Mallah, R. (2020). Toward Trustworthy AI Development: Mechanisms for Supporting Verifiable Claims. arXiv preprint arXiv:2004.07213.

Brynjolfsson, E., & McAfee, A. (2017). The Business of Artificial Intelligence: What it Can—and Cannot—Do for Your Organization. Harvard Business Review, 95(1), 63-76.

Crawford, K. (2016). Artificial Intelligence's White Guy Problem. The New York Times, 25.

Esteva, A., Kuprel, B., Novoa, R. A., Ko, J., Swetter, S. M., Blau, H. M., & Thrun, S. (2019). Dermatologist-level classification of skin cancer with deep neural networks. Nature, 542(7639), 115-118.

Floridi, L., Cowls, J., Beltrametti, M., Chatila, R., Chazerand, P., Dignum, V., ... &Vayena, E. (2018). AI4People—an ethical framework for a good AI society: Opportunities, risks, principles, and recommendations. Minds and Machines, 28(4), 689-707.

Hughes-Hassell, S., &Mancall, J. (2021). Advancing Equity in Public Libraries through Artificial Intelligence: A Report to the American Library Association. San José State University.

Jobin, A., Ienca, M., &Vayena, E. (2019). The global landscape of AI ethics guidelines. Nature Machine Intelligence, 1(9), 389-399.

Koedinger, K. R., Booth, J. L., & Klahr, D. (2012). Instructional complexity and the science to constrain it. Science, 337(6090), 165-166.

Lazer, D., Pentland, A., Adamic, L., Aral, S., Barabasi, A. L., Brewer, D., ... &Jebara, T. (2020). Computational social science: Obstacles and opportunities. Science, 369(6509), 1060-1062.

Lee, V. R., & Searson, M. (2020). Exploring the Educational Potential of AI in K-12 and Informal Learning Environments: Emerging Uses and Design Principles. Harvard Education Press.

Lillard, A. S., Lerner, M. D., Hopkins, E. J., Dore, R. A., Smith, E. D., & Palmquist, C. M. (2015). The impact of pretend play on children's development: A review of the evidence. Psychological Bulletin, 141(1), 1-34.

Russell, S. J., & Norvig, P. (2021). Artificial Intelligence: A Modern Approach. Pearson.

Rudin, C. (2019). Stop explaining black box machine learning models for high stakes decisions and use interpretable models instead. Nature Machine Intelligence, 1(5), 206-215.

Warschauer, M. (2019). Technology and Social Inclusion: Rethinking the Digital Divide. MIT Press.

Made in the USA
Columbia, SC
30 June 2025